An H
and Ge
Tour of

KILKERRAN
GRAVEYARD

by
Angus Martin

illustrated by
George John Stewart

KINTYRE CIVIC SOCIETY

Published by:
Kintyre Civic Society
and available from The Secretary at:
"Dunara",
Lochpark,
Carradale East,
Campbeltown,
Argyll,
PA28 6SG

Text set in Sabon by
Rowland Phototypesetting Ltd
and printed and bound by St Edmundsbury Press Ltd
Bury St Edmunds, Suffolk

INTRODUCTION

One evening in June, 2004, I found myself, for the first time, guiding a group of people around the beautiful grounds of Kilkerran grave-yard. Despite the heavy rain for most of that day, nearly 50 folk turned up, many more than I had expected . . . or desired. We coped, however, and the event – organised by The Kintyre Civic Society – appeared to be a success and has since been repeated.

Graveyards clearly fascinate many folk, myself included. Granted, there may be an element of the morbid, but there is much else to experience. Many inscriptions tell abbreviated stories, which a little research can expand; some offer philosophical advice, mostly Biblical; much implicit grief and tragedy will be encountered, cer-tainly, but there are also hidden depths of history, biography and genealogy, which I hope this work will partly reveal.

The main industries – farming, fishing, whisky-distilling, boat-building and shipping – are touched on, as are the main population elements: the early 'native' Gaelic families and the mutation of their names, the arrival of Lowland settlers in the seventeenth century and of Irish settlers in the nineteenth. Some cultural achievements are looked at, along with events and individuals of special interest.

I was asked, by the Civic Society, to write this book soon after the first tour and jumped at the chance, because a project of this kind had for years exercised my imagination and needed only a frame-work. A much bigger frame could have been used, but this, in the meantime, will have to suffice. If any reader has interesting informa-tion on individuals or families buried in Kilkerran, let me know and it might be possible to include entries in a revised or supplementary edition of this work.

The basic concept of this publication is scarcely new. Back in 1922, Colonel Charles Mactaggart delivered, to the Kintyre Antiquarian Society, a paper entitled *A Ramble Through the Old*

Kilkerran Graveyard, which was subsequently published and has long been out of print. I have chosen not to infringe on his territory, not only because he has already been there, but also because the oldest section has been effectively closed by Argyll & Bute Council owing to the unsafe condition of some of the monuments there.

The saint from whom Kilkerran takes its name is usually identified as the widely-venerated Ciaran, born about AD 515 and associated with the abbey of Clonmacnoise, which he founded shortly before his death in 548. John Marsden, however, in *Sea-Roads of the Saints*,[1] asserts that Ciaran of Clonmacnoise 'is nowhere recorded as having ever left Ireland', and that the Irish missionary in question was the earlier Ciaran of Saigir.

Whichever Ciaran is commemorated, his association with Campbeltown is based on two place-names. The first is *Ceann Loch Chille Chiarain*, or the Head of the Loch of Ciaran's Cell, which was – and is still – the Gaelic name for Campbeltown. The other is St Ciaran's Cave – at Auchenhoan Head, on the coast south of Campbeltown – which may have been a religious retreat of the saint.

Kilkerran church first appears on record in the mid-thirteenth century. The parish throughout the medieval period encompassed the eastern part of the peninsula between Campbeltown Loch and Balnabraid Glen, but, after the Reformation, the previously independent parishes of Kilmichael, Kilchousland and Kilkivan were joined to Kilkerran to form the united parish of Lochhead, afterwards Campbeltown.

The burial-ground has grown immensely since its expansion beyond the walls of the original churchyard. The first of the six additional divisions was in part acquired from the Presbytery of Kintyre (glebe land) and in part from the Duke of Argyll. It was purchased in 1856 by the Parochial Board, and the first interment there, a child of John Greenlees' of Stewarton, was in May 1857.[2] Expansion, both westward and southward, continued, as demand dictated, and this guidebook will utilise these divisions, though not in strict numerical order. The final division – at the western extremity – marks the limit of expansion, and the graves therein are the most recent.

In that division, though it is scarcely touched on here, will be found a progressively less formal approach to death and remembrance. Nick-names – such as 'Bonny', 'Tiger', 'Tucker' and 'Bud' – now appear in some strength, and the engraved imagery increasingly represents not the inspirational or consolatory – crosses, doves, hands clasped in prayer, etc. – but the plainly secular, particularly in the representation of hobbies and interests, such as golfing, angling, shooting, carpet-bowling, and bagpiping.

Kilkerran Cemetery has the distinction of being included in the Collins guide *Scotland the Best*. The 1998 edition remarks: 'Guess you could do worse than see Campbeltown and die.'

To enable readers to further study particular individuals and families, I have incorporated enumerated sources in the text, but much genealogical data, from my own files, is devoid of source-references in the interest of avoiding textual over-cluttering.

I have to thank, for particular assistance with this booklet: Murdo MacDonald, Argyll & Bute Archivist, Lochgilphead – now retired – for his invaluable input; my wife Judy, for computer and other assistance; Gloria Siggins, for information on military matters; George McSporran, for his company on so many convivial strolls around the graveyard; Alastair Campbell of Airds, Unicorn Pursuivant of Arms, for valued corrections to the penultimate draft, and all others – acknowledged individually in the references – who helped with particular entries.

Angus Martin
13 Saddell Street, Campbeltown,
Argyll PA28 6DN, Scotland

A Note on the Relationship
Between the Text and the Map

The numbered entries in the text correspond with the numbers on the accompanying fold-out map. Both map and text utilise the divisions, or walled sections, by which the cemetery has expanded over the past 150 years. Owing to the scale of the map, absolute precision has not been possible, but by careful orientation all the enumerated gravestones should be traceable, whether or not the reader strictly follows the sequence.

THE GRAVES

Division 1

1. KENNEDY. When I first noticed this headstone, standing in curious isolation outwith the west-facing wall of the old section, close to the main road, I assumed that John Kennedy had been a suicide and therefore denied burial in consecrated ground, a measure which also formerly applied to unbaptised children. Later, however, I was able to connect the date and location of his death with the loss of a Campbeltown smack, the *Mystery*, which foundered on Skerryvore reef, Machrihanish, while on passage to the drift-net herring-fishery in the 'North', or Minch, in May of 1869. The mishap, which proved fatal to the crew of seven, was indeed a mystery, because the weather had been fine that night. The conjecture

· KENNEDY ·   Fishing Smack 'MYSTERY' foundering on reef.

at the time was that the entire crew was sleeping below, with the exception of the helmsman, who must himself also have fallen asleep.

A Pans fisherman, Dugald McMillan, heading out to sea with one of his sons at about six o' clock in the morning, discovered four of the crew six miles offshore. They had attached themselves to net-buoys and were still afloat, but dead. At that time, many fishermen were unable to swim. Some subscribed to the fatalistic belief that if the sea was going to take you, then take you it would.

The smack's master, Dugald Mathieson, belonged to Campbeltown, while the crew was a mixture – typical for the time – of locals and hired hands from the Highlands and Islands, of which John Kennedy – from Applecross in Wester Ross – was one.[3]

2. **WALKER.** Nine stones along from No. 1, this stone – unusually, of polished slate – commemorates another local shipping tragedy, the foundering of the Campbeltown schooner *Moy* in 1884. Her master was John Walker, '. . . honest, straightforward, and brave to a fault . . . In his own profession he was excelled by none'. He had been awarded a '1st class silver medal' by Napoleon III of France for his 'marked bravery' in saving the crew of the French vessel *Jeune Heloise,* wrecked in Campbeltown Loch on 24 February, 1868.

Captain Walker's own command almost reached the safety of Campbeltown Loch during that 'most eventful period of storm and disaster'. She was seen approaching about 3 p.m. on 23 January, but was 'driven back by the hurricane violence of the wind'. The doomed schooner, 'bravely labouring in the tempest towards Pladda', was soon obscured by gathering darkness and storm-driven rain and spume, and was never seen again.

All hands perished: 56-year-old Captain Walker and two other Campbeltown men, the unmarried mate, 22-year-old Donald McInnes, and 23-year-old Hugh Robertson (no. 29); also Robert McCracken and another young man, shipped in Belfast, whose name was unknown at the time of the tragedy.[4]

Captain Walker appears in the Census of 1881 living at 2 Burnside Street with his wife, Sarah Carruthers, and eight children, ranging from 25-year-old Grace, a dressmaker, to three-year-old Jack. His parents (married 2/1/1821) were Neil Walker, shipmaster, and Mary McInnes – daughter of Donald McInnes, fisherman,

Dalintober – who are buried in Kilchousland with the McInnes family. The Walker family earlier belonged to Kilcalmonell Parish.

The *Moy* – 84 feet long, 22 feet of beam and with a draught of 9 feet – was the first vessel built by the Campbeltown Shipbuilding Company (no. 32). Her launch, on 20 March, 1878, attracted more than 3000 spectators, on land and on sea. She was built for the Dalaruan and Hazelburn distillery companies and named after her owners' estate to the west of Campbeltown. The christening was performed by Martha Greenlees, daughter of one of the owners, with a bottle of Campbeltown whisky 'gaily decorated with flowers'.[5]

3. MCCALLUM. Turn to right of path. John McCallum (died 19/1/1863) is described as 'Seaman on board H.M.R.C. Wickham'. The abbreviation represents 'Her Majesty's Revenue Cutter'. These fast, armed, sailing ships were stationed at Campbeltown to intercept international smugglers, and drew many of their crew-members from the local seafaring community. Most of the 'cutters-men' burials are in the old section, this one being an exception. Officers and men sometimes did extremely well from prize money. In May, 1821, the *Wickham* (Captain Beatson) captured an American schooner, loaded with contraband tobacco, off the Irish coast.[6] Her captain's share of the prize money, according to Col Charles Mactaggart, was reputed to be about £9000, an astronomical sum for that time.[7]

The families of such cutter captains as Henry Dundas Beatson, Thomas Lacy and James Melville – all buried close to one another in the old section – intermarried in the local community and the sur-names recur in Division 1. The cutters most closely associated with Campbeltown were the *Swift*, *Hardwick*, *Wellington* and *Wickham*, an 1825 painting of which, by Robert Salmon, is in storage at Campbeltown Museum. Captain Beatson built The Hall and Captain Lacy lived next door, in Springfield House, while Eagle Park on Low Askomil was built for Captain Melville. The fullest account of the Campbeltown Revenue Cutters appears in *A Ramble Through the Old Kilkerran Graveyard*, referred to in the Introduction. Duncan Campbell, father of Burns's 'Highland Mary', moved to Campbeltown from Cowal to take up employment in the Revenue Service (no. 31).

4. McCALLUM. Back to the left, and against the wall, another McCallum mariner and another shipwreck, that of the Campbeltown sloop *Jenny Lind*, which foundered off the coast of Arran on 2 October, 1860, taking with her, at the age of 40, her master Donald McCallum. When the storm broke at two o' clock in the morning – west-south-west, then veering north-west – the *Jenny Lind* was heading for her home port. The crew also drowned: William Mustard, who left a widow, Campbeltown-born Janet Clark, and four children,[8] and a 'young lad', William MacIntyre.[9] That great storm left in its wake much death and destruction across the west of Scotland.

The vessel has been perpetuated in the fishermen's place-name, Jenny Lind's Bay, north of Drumadoon, and her precise location on the seabed is still known to some of the older fishermen. That place-name also perpetuates the memory of the soprano after whom the boat was named. Jenny Lind – 'the Swedish Nightingale' – was born in Stockholm in 1820 and attained immense international celebrity. A 'paragon of art and beauty', she died in 1887, outlasting by some 26 years her maritime namesake.

MacCallum – an ecclesiastical name, from Gaelic *Mac Ghille Chaluim*, Devotee of Saint Columba – has for long been one of the most common of Kintyre surnames, and it is generally accepted that members of the clan settled Kintyre, from their homeland in Mid Argyll, following the seventeenth century Campbell ascendancy here.

Mary McEachran, Donald McCallum's widow, survived until 1900. She bore one of the oldest and most interesting of the native names in Kintyre. It derives from *Mac Each-thighearna*, Son of the Horse Lord, and its origins arguably reach back into pagan totemism.[10]

Campbeltown-born Professor Duncan McEachran (1841–1924) of McGill University, Montreal, was a world authority in veterinary science, specialising – aptly enough – in horse diseases. He was also an avid horse-breeder and imported many Kintyre Clydesdales to his ranch in the Western Plains of Canada.[11]

The exquisite medieval cross which stands at the foot of Main Street, Campbeltown, was carved for Ivor MacEachern, who was probably parson at Kilkivan in the late fourteenth century; and one of the two late fifteenth century cross-shafts near the entrance to

McCallum. — Shipwreck of Campbeltown sloop "Jenny Lind"

Kilkerran Cemetery was dedicated to Colin MacEachern – thought to be chief of the MacEacherns or MacEachrans of Killellan until the early sixteenth century – and his wife Katerina.[12]

A tradition of how the MacEachrans arrived in Kintyre (in the twelfth century) is preserved in 'The Manuscript History of Craignish'.[13] Craignish is said to have come into the possession of the Campbells through the *toiseach*, or chief, of the MacEachrans having granted the lands to Dugald Campbell, whom he had fostered. MacEachran, accompanied by a retinue of friends and followers, then set off for Ireland 'resolveing to establish a new Collonie' and swearing that he would 'rest and take up his residence wherever the buckling ropes or wreaths of his bagadge first broke'. That propitious event occurred at Killellan, and 'he and his followers unsheathd their swords and without furder Ceremonie dispossest the possessor by force of arms'.

5. SMITH. Cross diagonally to the right of the path and find a cross with angel affixed, her right hand pointing heavenward. Captain Donald Smith, a mariner well-known in his time, is buried here with his wife Janet McEachen Carmichael. Captain Smith belonged to Gigha, but as a boy moved with his parents – Peter Smith and Janet McGougan – to Campbeltown and later settled in Dalintober. His

·SMITH·. Sir Thomas Lipton's 'SHAMROCK I'.

first command was a coasting vessel co-owned with his father, but c. 1869 he was given command of a local schooner, the *Mary Colville*, and later became master of another local schooner, the *Finlaggan*, in which he engaged extensively in foreign trade for more than 20 years, sailing to North America, the Mediterranean and the Baltic. Despite crossing the Atlantic many times in the *Finlaggan*, he suffered no mishap, though his hard weather exploits were the talk of the fishermen at Dalintober weigh-house.

When the *Finlaggan* was sold about 1896, Captain Smith found employment as a yacht-master. Such, indeed, was his reputation that he was invited, in 1899, to navigate Sir Thomas Lipton's *Shamrock I* across to New York, for Lipton's first attempt to 'wrest the America's Cup from the Yankees'. The offer, however, was 'modestly declined'.[14]

Captain Smith died at the age of 69 on 2/6/1902, not 1903 as the gravestone inscription has it. His seaman brother Archibald (died 1897, aged 60) and wife Mary Martin (died 1919, aged 74), with other family members, are buried alongside. Given their Gaelic background, Smith may be assumed to represent *Mac a ghobhainn*, Son of the smith, also represented by McGown, which in South Kintyre is likely to be of nineteenth century Irish origin.

Captain Donald's wife Janet's name, Carmichael, almost certainly represents Gaelic *Mac Ghille Mhicheil*, one of the many ecclesiastical surnames which have been obscured. In the eighteenth and nineteenth centuries, the name Carmichael was prominent in Skipness Parish, but appears, by migration, in Campbeltown Parish in the nineteenth century, particularly in the fishing community at Dalintober. These Carmichaels have disappeared in name, though their genes persist. The present Carmichael family here has its origins in the Island of Mull.

6. STALKER. Against the north wall, an imposing three-panelled McMurchy monument which proclaims: 'BLESSED ARE THE DEAD THAT DIE IN THE LORD.' On the right-hand panel – eroding rapidly – appears Donald Stalker (died 18/9/1919), by reason of his marriage to Elizabeth McMurchy (died 29/3/1923). They produced a very talented and long-lived family, which included two daughters, Kate (1870–1956) and Lizzie (1876–1970), who were teachers at Campbeltown Grammar School, and two sons who were writers – commemorated on separate stones – Archibald Kelly McMurchy (1882–1984) and Neil Sinclair (1886–1980).

Archibald was educated at Campbeltown Grammar School, passed, at the age of 17, the Civil Service Entrance Examination, and moved to London. By 1924 he was employed in the Scottish Board of Health in Edinburgh, was a contributor to *The Spectator* and *Cornhill Magazine*, had published his *Intimate Life of Sir Walter Scott* and a collection of verse, titled simply *Poems*. In an interview with a national newspaper, he distanced himself, unusually for the time, from the militaristic history of his race: 'I lose no opportunity of proclaiming my Gaelic descent, though it is one of my real regrets that so imaginative and artistic a race as ours should have so long wasted itself on clan feuds, Jacobite rebellions and foreign wars.'[15]

Neil, better known by his middle name 'Sinclair', was fifth son and tenth child of Donald Stalker and Elizabeth McMurchy, as his stone records. He too was a writer, though little of his work has been published (see, however, his youthful account of 'A Trip to Carradale, 1902' in *The Kintyre Magazine*, No. 55). Family tradition records that he got his middle name from a great-grandfather, Peter Sinclair (1788–1863), who 'was press-ganged in Campbeltown and fought at Trafalgar in 1805, coming home with a fair amount of prize money'.

In his early twenties, Sinclair emigrated to Canada with his brother Donald, returning to Europe with the Canadian army to fight in the Great War, an experience which yielded the interesting, but as yet unpublished, memoir, 'New Year's Eve of Victory in Brussels, 1918'. On demobilisation, he returned to Canada and was granted land by the government. This consisted of part of Gabriola Island, off Vancouver. It was largely rough woodland, which Sinclair worked hard to clear and farm, and which, as Vancouver prospered and expanded, he sold, returning in the 1960s to Campbeltown, where he married an old friend, Dorothy Harvey (died 20/03/2002) with whom he eventually settled in Marchwood, Glenramskill.

One of the most colourful characters of twentieth century Campbeltown, 'London Kate', belonged to the same Stalker family. She was born in Southend, where her father Duncan was a postman, but brought up by her paternal grandmother, Katie McMillan Stalker, at the Flush, near Campbeltown, after he was thrown from his gig and killed near Gartvaigh in 1869.[16] Her grandfather had a stone erected in Kilkerran, close to Number 4 in this account, but all that it says is: '1879/ Erected by/Donald Stalker/Flush'. The rest is blank and now lichen-covered. In her late teens, Kate travelled to London – hence her nick-name – and found employment there in domestic service. In 1924, soon after returning to Campbeltown, she married John McCorkindale, who died in 1942. Her status as a local 'worthy' was established during the period when she ran a tea-room in Main Street, and consolidated after she took charge of MacBrayne's bus office, a duty to which she applied a legendary iron rule and only retired from at the age of 80. For an account of her idiosyncratic life, see *The Kintyre Magazine*, No. 52.

Kate died at the age of 93, another long-lived Stalker. As we have seen, Archibald lived to the age of 101 and Neil Sinclair to 93, and there were others whose longevity was remarked on. Neil Stalker in Rhunahaorine was 98 when he died in 1888[17] and Barbara Stalker – Mrs Neil Hyndman – 95 years old when she died at Skipness in 1927.[18] The name Stalker, which was mainly associated with north Kintyre, derives from *Mac an Stocair*, possibly Son of the Trumpeter, but see my *Kintyre: The Hidden Past*.[19]

7. MACKEICH. Though a McCallum gravestone, the chief interest here is Edward McCallum's wife, Agnes MacKeich, who died

11/12/1893. The progenitor of this family, according to tradition, was a Jacobite Keith from Aberdeenshire, who fled to Kintyre after the Battle of Culloden in 1746, settling first at Grianan, Carradale, then moving to Arnicle, at the head of Barr Glen, where an Archibald MacKeich is recorded in 1797–8.

Agnes was born there, and when she came to Campbeltown as a young girl she was a monoglot Gaelic speaker. She and Edward kept a public house near the junction of Longrow and Roading; she lived there for more than 60 years. By 1922, it was the last thatched house in Campbeltown. When she died at the age of 100 – as recorded in the register of deaths – she was survived by three sons and three daughters, 23 grandchildren and 18 great-grandchildren.

The last of the family in Kintyre were the brothers Duncan (born 1887) and John (born 1889), retired farmers, who used the form 'MacKeith'. They were born at Sunadale – sons of Duncan MacKeith and Catherine McArthur – and, when they died at Saddell in the penultimate decade of the twentieth century, were numbered with the few remaining native Gaelic speakers in Kintyre.[20]

Confusingly, if these MacKeichs/MacKeiths were originally Keiths, then the nineteenth and twentieth century Keiths were originally MacKeichs! The name is supposed to represent Gaelic *Mac Shithic*, 'Son of the Wolf', but there is reason to believe that some MacKeich/MacKeith/Keith families in Kintyre were properly Mac-Kichan/MacEachan/MacEachine, from the Gaelic personal name *Eachunn*, usually anglicised as 'Hector'. On 4 June, 1902, Robert McKeich – a New Zealand soldier whose father, James, was born in Campbeltown – became the last Allied fatality of the Boer War.[21]

8. McGRORY. A nineteenth century Irish immigrant family, but not a typical one, because most such families which remained in Campbeltown – e.g., Black, Broadley/Brodie, Durnan/Durnin, Finn, McKay, Meenan, Morans/Morrans, Newlands and O'Hara – were almost exclusively involved in fishing. Anthony McGrory (died 12/10/1901, aged 79), a quarryman, and his wife Isabella Rafferty (died 31/7/1905, aged 79), both born in County Down, were settled in Campbeltown by 1845, and their children were all born here.

Sons Dennis and Charles were active amateur photographers between 1890 and 1910. When their collection was donated to Campbeltown Library by Charles's son, A. P. McGrory – a promi-

McGRORY.

Dennis and Charles McGrory – photographers.

nent businessman and Provost of Campbeltown from 1959 to 1964 – it comprised some 3000 negatives and glass lantern slides. The original glass negatives and prints are held at Argyll and Bute Library Service Headquarters in Dunoon, and digitised images from the collection can be viewed at Campbeltown Library. Now known as 'The McGrory Collection', it is a pictorial resource of national significance and perhaps the greatest cultural achievement of the Irish community in Kintyre.

John, another son of Anthony and Isabella, established the 11-acre nursery, a part of which lands – discreetly gifted to the community by his daughter, Cissie – is now occupied by the health centre and hospital.[22]

'McGrory' represents Irish *Mac Ruaidhri*, Son of Rory.

9. McDOUGALL. This stone was raised in 1871 to commemorate Barbara McIsaac, wife of John McDougall, clothier in Campbeltown. Of this McDougall family nothing is so far known. MacDougall was not one of the old Kintyre family names – such as MacDonald, MacEachran, MacKay, MacAlister and MacNeill – but belonged in North Argyll. The MacDougall families at present in Kintyre have disparate origins.

There have been MacIsaacs in South Kintyre since at least the early sixteenth century. From the seventeenth to the nineteenth century, the name was associated particularly with the Learside – Feochaig and Corphin farms – and a branch became prominent as boat-owners and fishermen in nineteenth century Campbeltown.

The particular interest in this stone, however, is the death in January, 1919, of John Allan Watson – a grandson of John McDougall – 'while on active service in North Russia'. He was, in fact – as research by Mrs Gloria Siggins, Carradale, disclosed – murdered by a deranged US serviceman.

Some time in the 1880s, Watson's mother, Helen McDougall, met and married Robert Wilson Watson – from Killyleagh, County Down, Ireland – who had come to Campbeltown as a young Excise officer. John Allan Watson was born at Broughty Ferry in 1888 and educated in Paisley and Glasgow. He joined the Army Reserve in 1915, was called up into the Glasgow Yeomanry and soon afterwards transferred to the 2nd Battalion Scottish Rifles and sent to France in December 1916. After a couple of months at the front, he was recalled to join the Royal Artillery Cadet School at St John's Wood Barracks, London, and spent the remainder of 1917 training in the UK.

In February 1918, he was commissioned 2nd Lieutenant in the Royal Field Artillery, and in July sailed for Russia with an Allied expeditionary force to assist the White Russians against the Bolshevik revolutionaries. On 31 January, 1919, at Smolny Barracks, Archangel, he was shot dead by 22-year-old Private Frank O'Callaghan, serving with the Medical Detachment, 339th US Infantry. The motive for Watson's murder was never satisfactorily explained, but O'Callaghan was subsequently diagnosed as suffering from dementia praecox and repatriated to a hospital for the insane. Lieut Watson was interred in Obozerskaya Burial Ground, Archangel. He was, in Gloria Siggins's summation, 'tragically in the wrong place at the wrong time'.[23]

Division 2

10. **GRANTHAM.** There are, in Kilkerran, several graves of the children of Customs and Excise families which came to

. GRANTHAM .

Henry Grantham in the uniform
of the local Rifle Volunteers.

Campbeltown during the whisky boom of the nineteenth and the
early twentieth centuries. These graves are among the most
poignant, because in all cases the families moved on, perhaps never
to return. Mary and Margaret Forrester, Willie and George Gordon
Ross, Maggie May Moore, Lizzie McGoldrick and George Ellis
Grantham are among those children. Young George was born and
died here – on 24/9/1885, aged 18 months – of measles, followed by

bronchitis and finally convulsions. The stone bears the words: 'A Parting Token.'

His father, Henry Grantham, a native of Newark, came to Campbeltown from Retford in England in 1882 with his family – wife Elizabeth Tomlinson and sons Henry, William and Charles – and remained until 1886, when transferred to Lancaster. His two brothers were also employed in the Customs and Excise Service and were, like him, strict teetotal Methodists! A picture survives of Henry in the uniform of the local Rifle Volunteers, complete with kilt and glengarry, and with rifle held at his side. The family also inherited Henry's gauge, a brass-hinged rod marked off in hogsheads, butts, puncheons, firkins, etc.[24]

Excisemen – who collected Government excise, or duty, on whisky, and in earlier, more lawless times, were tasked with apprehending illicit distillers and smugglers – were known as gaugers, locally 'gadgers'. Tangy Place, at the east end of High Street, was formerly known as 'the Gadgers' Berracks', or 'barracks', from the Excisemen quartered there, and a rock beyond Trench Point was 'the Gadger's Rock', from one who regularly bathed there.

As indicators of the level of Excise presence here, *Pigot's Directory* for 1837 lists 31 'Excise Office' employees in Campbeltown, and the List of Voters for the Burgh in 1890 includes two Supervisors and 26 Officers of Inland Revenue.[25] Excise families – predominantly from England and Ireland – swelled the membership of the Scottish Episcopal Church in Campbeltown. Indeed, of the eight committee members elected in 1848 to provide a stipend for the Episcopal clergyman, secure a temporary church and – in the longer term – a permanent church, four were Officers of Excise: Walter Hore, Thomas Rack, Thomas Nicholson and Edward Scattergood.[26]

11. FLEMING. This impressive monument, set against the north wall, bears only one name, that of Alexander Fleming – 'Ironmaster, Glasgow' – who died unmarried in Glasgow on 16/10/1909. Fabulously wealthy, he left an estate worth £768,420 9s 6d, which, in present-day values, would surely put him into the multimillionaire bracket. Yet, he was a rather private man, his chief delight being in 'the quietness and seclusion of his own home, where favoured friends could always find him at his best'. Of hobbies he had few, but he enjoyed a 'great fondness' for whist.

FLEMING.
Alexander Fleming — Ironmaster.

Of seventeenth century Lowland Plantation stock, he was born in 1824 at Ballievain Farm, which as early as 1666 was occupied by one James Fleming. Captain John Fleming, R.N. (1772–1849), who belonged to the same family, had a distinguished naval career, from which he retired with honours in 1816. Captain Fleming, who is buried in the old section, acquired Muasdale and Glencreggan, among other properties, after his retirement, and built Fleming's Land on Castlehill, Campbeltown,[27] which property Alexander subsequently restored and improved.

Some misfortune in Alexander's young life is hinted at in his obituary, for he was 'early thrown upon his own resources'. Following a parish schooling locally, he moved to Glasgow in 1837 and there attended night classes and assiduously 'cultivated his faculties'. After a period as an independent iron-merchant, Alexander was invited to join the firm of Messrs William Baird & Co., iron and coal masters, Glasgow, as its commercial manager, and ultimately became a partner.

'Almost to the last he maintained his great shrewdness, keen mother-wit, and strong commonsense, qualities which had stood him in great stead in his career . . . Few bubble schemes could stand his careful and studied examination, and his success as a salesman was known to all members of his business circle.'

Some six years before his death, Alexander suffered a 'paralytic shock' which limited his active involvement in the business of the company. He acquired the estate of Kilmaho in 1872 and that of Oatfield in 1890. He gave financial assistance in the restoration of the old Lowland church in Kirk Street and in the formation of Longrow South, and 'no good cause ever appealed to him in vain'. In the year before his death he was presented with the freedom of the burgh.[28]

Among other eminent locally-born industrialists may be mentioned John Colville (1844–1924) of the Glasgow Cotton Spinning Co Ltd., James Templeton (1802–85), carpet-manufacturer, of James Templeton & Co, Glasgow, and David Colville (1813–98), iron and steel master and founder of David Colville & Sons, Motherwell.[29] David Colville is the ancestor of the present Lord Clydesmuir, whose grandfather, the 1st Baron, was Secretary of State for Scotland and Governor of Bombay.

Division 1

12. **MACKINNON.** The Celtic-style cross surmounting this grave has been broken at base and head of its shaft. Its inscription, to Dr

Campbell MacKinnon MD CB, who died 2/3/1871, states his professional distinctions: Inspector General of Hospitals, Bengal Army, and Honorary Physician to Queen Victoria. He also distinguished himself, by his courage and devotion to duty, during the military campaigns in which he was involved: the Afghan War, from 1839 to 1842, and the later Indian Mutiny of 1857–58 (see also Carmichael, no. 35). For those readers unimpressed by services to Empire, MacKinnon was a discreet and generous friend to the poor of the town. 'It is seldom indeed,' his obituarist remarked, 'that all classes of the community unite so heartily in lamenting a removal from their midst.'[30]

`Dr MacKinnon was not, however, a native of Kintyre. As with both his parents, he was born in Arran. His father, the Rev John Campbell MacKinnon, was the son of a farmer, Duncan MacKinnon, while his mother, Isabella Fullarton – daughter of Lewis Fullarton of Kilmichael[31] – was born into an old landed family.

Dr MacKinnon married the youngest daughter* of Captain Henry Dundas Beatson, two of whose sons served with him as medical officers in India. That distinguished Campbeltown family produced Sir George Beatson, whose name is perpetuated in the Beatson Oncology Centre in the Western Infirmary and the Beatson Institute for Cancer Research in Bearsden, where hangs a portrait of George Beatson, in his youth, as assistant to Lord Lister, the 'father of antiseptic surgery'.[32]

MacKinnon is the anglicised form of Gaelic *Mac Fhionghuin* and was interchangeable in Kintyre with MacKinven (no. 20). I have been told that the family origin of the international capitalist, Sir William MacKinnon, born in Campbeltown in 1823 and buried at Clachan in 1893, was also Arran.

13. MACTAGGART. The best-known Kintyre McTaggart is, of course, the painter William (1835–1910), whose great-grandparents Edward McIntaggart (c.1715–94) and Margaret Stewart are buried at Kilkenzie. The other notable family of the name in South Kintyre – no connection between the two families has yet been established, but the possibility remains – descends from Malcolm McIntaggart, who is buried in the old section and whose stone describes him as 'farmer,

---

*Neither she nor their son appears in the inscription.

Craigag', which is a township on the deserted Atlantic coast south of Machrihanish. Malcolm died in 1738, at an unknown age.

There is, hereabouts, a cluster of Mactaggart family stones, but I have chosen, as the focus, the neighbouring monuments to Charles Rowatt Mactaggart and his son Henry Dundas Beatson Mactaggart, whose potted histories materialise later.

That Mactaggart family is best known for its remarkably long history of legal practice in Campbeltown. The firm was founded in 1810 by Daniel Mactaggart, Kilkivan, and is represented, four generations on, by the former senior partner, and now consultant, John Norman Mactaggart.

Daniel Mactaggart married Christian Hamilton Campbell, daughter of Lieutenant Scipio Duroure Campbell, of the 100th Regiment of Foot (who belonged to a cadet branch of the Campbells of Inverawe and married Gilles, daughter of Archibald Campbell, of the Bragleenmore family, sometime Chamberlain of Kintyre).[33] Their eldest son, Scipio Mactaggart, practised for a time with the firm, then moved to Inveraray and became Sheriff Clerk of Argyll, Provost of the Burgh and a talented amateur photographer. Another son, John Daniel, emigrated to Australia and founded a farming dynasty, which later expanded into many branches of commerce.

The youngest son, Charles Rowatt (died 1/2/1882, aged 54) represents the second generation of family lawyers. He married Margaret Stewart Beatson (died 23/2/1907, aged 82), daughter of Captain Henry Dundas Beatson (nos. 3 & 12). Charles was named after an uncle, Dr Charles Rowatt Mactaggart, whose unenviable lot it was to deal with the cholera epidemic which struck Campbeltown in 1832.

Henry Dundas Beatson Mactaggart, the eldest son of Charles and Margaret Mactaggart, spent 30 years in India with the British India Steam Navigation Company. He devoted his retirement in Campbeltown to public service, but died – at Rosemount, on 16/11/1912, aged 59 – just eight days after his election as Provost. As his stone records, he married one Alice Moscardi. She was daughter of an Italian priest, Lucio Donato Moscardi, and an aristocratic Czech, Louisa von Sal. After Henry's death, Alice left Campbeltown and died at Alassio, on the Italian Riviera, in 1934. Their youngest daughter, Basil Hamilton Mactaggart – Basil Hamilton was her maternal grandmother, wife of Captain Beatson – married a major

17

in the Indian Army, Ivan L O'Hare, and, as the stone records, died at
Port Sudan in 1929 at the age of 37.

To return, however, to the central theme – which is the legal succession – the second son of Charles Rowatt Mactaggart, Daniel
Campbell Mactaggart, held all the offices his father before him had
held: he was procurator-fiscal for Kintyre for 44 years, town clerk
and agent for the Commercial Bank.

A third son, Colonel Charles Mactaggart CSI CIE, had a distinguished career in the Indian Medical Service and became,
among other prestigious appointments, Inspector General of Indian
Prisons. In his retirement in Campbeltown, he became a noted local
historian, whose books – including **A Ramble Through the Old**
Kilkerran Graveyard – are still consulted.

The youngest son, John Norman Mactaggart, formed, with his
brother Dan, the third of the legal generations. He commanded the
1st Argyll Highland Rifle Volunteers, in which he served for some 20
years.

John Norman's elder son, Charles (1898–1984) – the fourth
generation in the firm of C & D Mactaggart – enlisted in the 8th
Battalion Argyll & Sutherland Highlanders at the age of 17, was
awarded the MC for conspicuous bravery at Cambrai in November,
1917, and ultimately attained the rank of Captain. On his return to
Campbeltown, he practised as a solicitor until the age of 85, by
which time his son John had joined the firm.[34]

MacTaggart represents Gaelic *Mac an t-sagairt*, Son of the priest –
the marrying of priests was formerly tolerated – and the early forms
of the name in Kintyre follow that form, e.g. Donald Mcintagrt in
Auchork (Oatfield) in 1694 and Neil MacIntaggart in Dailclachan
(Lossit) in 1797.

14. **MITCHELL.** Here, side by side, lie two brothers – John and
William Mitchell – who prospered when Campbeltown was whisky
capital of the world, and whose legacy, Springbank Distillery, is
internationally renowned as a producer of superlative malt whisky.
Upwards of 35 Campbeltown distilleries are recorded, of which 20
survived into the twentieth century, which, however, brought with
it the decline and ultimately the collapse of the industry here.
Consider, though, that in the peak year of whisky-production in
Campbeltown, 1897, 1,810,226 gallons of the stuff were produced –

MITCHELL · John and William – Whisky Distillers

enough to kill outright the present population of Scotland! Those distilleries employed hundreds of men: making the whisky, coopering, cutting and carting the peat that dried and flavoured the malt, shipping in barley from markets as distant as the Baltic, and shipping out the whisky itself in barrels.

The Mitchell family belonged to Lowland stock planted in South Kintyre in the seventeenth century, and its members were largely tenant-farmers before entering the developing whisky business. John and William purchased Springbank Distillery in 1837 and remained together until c 1872, when the partnership was dissolved. John retained Springbank, while William built Glengyle Distillery – now owned by J & A Mitchell & Co Ltd and once again in production, as 'Kilkerran' – and later (1881) bought Rieclachan Distillery.

John was a town councillor for several years and also a director of the Campbeltown and Glasgow Steamboat Company. Upon his death in 1892, he left a widow – Mary Wylie (1818–1913) – two sons, seven daughters and an estate ultimately valued at £43,217. William (1819–87) was also a town councillor, for about 12 years, a member of the United Presbyterian Church and, politically, a Liberal, 'but never intolerant or extreme in his views'. His wife was Helen Greenlees (1822–1901) – another Lowland name – and he was survived by two sons and three daughters. His estate was valued at £15,803 19s 10d in 1888.[35]

Lt. Col. Colin 'Mad Mitch' Mitchell, who gained fame as commanding officer of the 1st Battalion The Argyll & Sutherland Highlanders, was of Argyll stock: his family came from Lochgilphead, but its Mitchell roots were in Kintyre. He realised a lifetime's ambition by joining the 8th Argylls in Italy at the end of the Second World War. Thereafter, he saw active service in Palestine, Korea, Cyprus and Borneo before leading his Battalion in the epic retaking of Crater in Aden in July, 1967. During this period, he made a point of choosing as his personal bodyguard another Mitchell, from Campbeltown: Corporal Hughie.[36] Colin Mitchell's autobiography, *Having Been a Soldier*, was published in 1969.

15. WALLACE. Two nineteenth century headstones commemorate members of this family which came to Kintyre in the seventeenth century with the Marquess of Argyll's settlement of Protestant Lowlanders, after the final fires of Clan Donald resistance in Kintyre were extinguished at Dunaverty and in the punitive aftermath of that slaughter (no. 31). The progenitor of the Kintyre Wallaces was Colonel James Wallace of Auchans in South Ayrshire, whose family was connected with that of the Scottish patriot Sir William Wallace.

Andrew McKerral has described Colonel Wallace as 'perhaps the most interesting of all the Lowland lairds who came to Kintyre'. A professional soldier, he was twice captured in battle – at Kilsyth in

1645 and at Dunbar in 1650 – and afterwards imprisoned. In 1666, after a relatively quiet period in Kintyre, he commanded the defeated Covenanting army at Rullion Green. Thereafter, under sentence of death, he chose exile and died in Rotterdam in 1678. The Kintyre Wallaces descend from Colonel James's sons, James and John.[37]

The earliest Wallace stone in the old graveyard is to John Wallace (died 1686). In the same plot are Thomas Wallace (1764–1820), Tirfergus, and his wife Janet Craig, parents of the William Wallace (1793–1865) on the southern stone here. William married Elizabeth McNair of Little Strath. In 1841, he took a sub-lease of West Drumlemble from the Campbeltown Coal Company, and 10 years later got the lease direct from the Duke of Argyll. Of their children, six emigrated to New Zealand and were among the pioneers in the Mangere area, only William (1826–97) – northern stone – remaining in Kintyre. He married Elizabeth Armour, a member of another prominent Lowland Plantation family, and diversified into the upholstery business, having served an apprenticeship locally with Robert Watson.[38] In 1883, he was advertising his services as 'upholsterer, paperhanger and cabinetmaker'.

West Drumlemble remained in the Wallace family until 2005, farmed by William's great-grandsons, William and James. The last of the Wallaces of Machribeg, Southend, whence the present Wallace family stemmed, emigrated to Ohio, USA, in the mid-nineteenth century.[39]

The firm of R. A. Wallace & Sons, Longrow – acquired by Robertson's Electrical Ltd. in 1996 – was founded by a son of William Jr's, Robert (1871–1943), who married Susan Clark. As well as being cabinetmakers and upholsterers, the firm earlier provided an undertaking service.

16. WEIR. In the hollow, against the south wall, this is unquestionably one of the most poignant memorials in the entire cemetery. Infant mortality was rife prior to the medical and sanitary advances which the twentieth century brought, and many inscriptions relate – albeit with utter inadequacy – the heartbreaking loss of child after child to illnesses and diseases which can now be routinely prevented or treated.

The Rev Walter Weir was minister of the Lowland Church from 1854 to 1864. In December of 1863, the year before his death, four

·WEIR·

4 OF REV. WEIR'S CHILDREN DIED AFTER DRINKING WATER FROM THE DUCHESS WELL.

of his six young children – Robert, Agnes, James and Walter – died, one after the other, of typhoid, after drinking water from the Duchess's Well at Castlehill Manse gate. That well was named after Elizabeth Tollemache – wife of Archibald Campbell, 1st Duke of Argyll – who often walked from her home at Limecraigs House along the tree-lined avenue to Castlehill Manse, there to visit her friend, the Rev James Boes, minister of the Lowland Church from 1694.[40]

Walter Weir was born in Glasgow in 1824 and educated at the University of Glasgow. He married, in 1854, Elizabeth, daughter of James Lamb of Aberlady, Midlothian. She remarried in 1872, and gained, I hope, some happiness and contentment after the traumas of that earlier decade. Of the two surviving children, it is known that Jessie Eliza, born in 1858, married Samuel Greenlees; but what became of James, born in 1860, remains uncertain.[41]

17. MACMILLAN. This is one of the most common names in Campbeltown and is found throughout Kintyre. The choice of a representative stone has, therefore, been more difficult than usual, but this stone is perhaps most apposite, since it represents one connected with Kilkerran Farm, which is next to the graveyard. It commem-

orates Hugh Macmillan (died 18/7/1977, aged 95) and his wife Anne Carmichael (died 16/3/1981, aged 81). Hugh's father, John, was born in Southend, on the farm of Knockmorain (now part of Coledrain), and settled in Kilkerran in 1870 with his bride, Agnes Reid of Kildavie. John's early potatoes – invariably the first in the local market – enjoyed a wide reputation for their quality.[42]

John and Agnes had four daughters and five sons, one of whom, Andrew, subsequently farmed Kilkerran, with assistance from Hugh, who began his career in the Assessor's Office, Campbeltown, and finished it as Assistant County Treasurer. His great love, however, was the land, and, before and after work, he helped at home with farm work and in the market garden with his sister, Margaret.

Margaret was the subject of a William McTaggart portrait, which hung above the fireplace in the artist's studio, and was said to have been his favourite work. That painting was originally titled 'Through the Barley', became 'Within a Mile of Campbeltown' and finally 'Maggie Macmillan – Fishergirl.' Mrs Barbara Wilkie remembers her aunt Margaret's telling of 'her mother brushing her long auburn hair before sitting on a little stool for Mr McTaggart in the parlour'.[43]

In 1930, Hugh married Anne, daughter of Archie Carmichael, fisherman in Dalintober. Their son John, also interred here, farmed Summerhill, Whitehill and Kilkerran until his death in 1996 at the age of 60. He was a well-known breeder of Arab horses, two of which, racing at Aintree in 1991, came in first and third.[44]

MacMillan represents Gaelic *Mac Mhaolain*, Son of the Tonsured, and implies monastic origin. Steer and Bannerman[45] postulate that the MacMillans may have been expelled from their lands a few years after Knapdale was forfeited to the crown by John, Lord of the Isles, in 1475. Certainly, members of the family appear in the Kintyre rentals compiled in 1505, 1506 and 1541, and Andrew McKerral remarks that 'MacMillans were among the most extensive occupiers of land in Kintyre in the sixteenth century'.[46] That the clan's earlier influence, in Knapdale, had waned, is apparent in the absence of MacMillan protagonists in the turbulent military and political events of the sixteenth and seventeenth centuries. The name also took the form *Mac Ghille Mhaoil*, as in 'Angus McIlvoil or McMillan' in the Old Parish Registers of Campbeltown (birth of his son Donald) on 26/11/1811. The name MacMillan in Campbeltown itself is probably mostly of nineteenth century Irish immigrant origin.

Malcolm McMillan – who was born in 1831 at Tangy and died at Millknowe, Campbeltown, in 1903 – emigrated to the United States as a young man and served in the Union Army throughout the Civil War (1861–65) for which he received a lifetime's pension of 2s a day from the US Government.[47]

Daniel MacMillan – whose pen-name was 'Dalintober', where he was born in 1845 – began his working life as an apprentice iron-monger in Campbeltown and later, in partnership with a brother, became a manufacturer of glass-paper and emery-cloth in Glasgow. He was also a published poet of some merit, as demonstrated in the controlled sentiment of 'The faces a' hae changed', which ends: 'In fancy's bower wi' vanished bliss/ On time I'll be avenged,/ Where a' remains unchanged to me,/ Where a' remains unchanged.'[48] Daniel, whose grandparents were John Macmillan and Anne Langwill in Coledrain, was of the same Macmillan family as that in Kilkerran.[49]

Major Duncan McMillan – born in Campbeltown in 1920 and founder in 1955 of the firm of house furnishers and flooring con-tractors in Longrow – won his Military Medal as a Sergeant with the 8th Argyll & Sutherland Highlanders during the desperate battle of Longstop Hill in Tunisia in 1943.

Alexander McMillan and Mary Ann Galbraith, the grandparents of Glasgow-born playwright, Hector MacMillan – *The Rising* (1970), *The Sash* (1973), etc. – belonged to Campbeltown.

The author of the Harry Potter novels, J. K. Rowling, can also claim a Kintyre ancestor – a maternal great-great-great grandfather was Dugald MacMillan of Lephenstrath, Southend.[50]

Division 2

18. FERGUSON. This stone, to James Ferguson (1847–1929) and his wife Agnes F Black (1869–1939), also commemorates their son Hugh Ferguson BSc FRSE (1912–1996), who was internationally recognised as 'one of the greatest scientific authorities on tropical agriculture' and a botanist 'whose expertise in tea was generally acknowledged as being among the best of the post-war era'.[51] He was born at Barlea Farm and educated at Campbeltown Grammar

FERGUSON. Tea-gathering in Nepal.

School, whence he went to Glasgow University to read Pure Botany and Agricultural Botany, graduating in 1934 with a first class honours degree.

Most of his working life was spent overseas – in Asia, Africa, the Middle East, the Far East and the Caribbean – and from 1967 he played an integral role in the tea interests of James Finlay and associated companies, which led to appointments, in 1969 and 1970, to the boards of Finlay's various companies. Following his retirement, in 1982, from his non-executive directorships, he returned to Campbeltown and immersed himself in the extensive garden at his home, Beach Hill, Low Askomil. He was President of the Kintyre Antiquarian and Natural History Society and in 1966 was elected a Fellow of the Royal Society of Edinburgh. His marriage to his first wife, Margaret McQuitty, who died in 1977, produced one son, Lieutenant-Commander Nicholas Hugh Ferguson, R. N. Hugh remarried, to Sarah Irwin Elkin MA (Edinburgh), in 1977.[52]

James, his father, was born in Campbeltown Parish and farmed first South Kilmaho and then Barlea, Glenbarr. His wife, Agnes Ferguson Black, was born at Dalkeith Farm, Glenbarr, daughter of Archibald Black and Mary Johnston, whose mother was Agnes Ferguson, of the same family as James.

No connection has yet been established between James Ferguson's family and the Ferguson family of builders, one of whom, Alexander, in July 1880, won, at Wimbledon, the National Rifle Association's most prestigious award, the annual Queen's Prize. Alexander was then about 28 years old and in partnership with his father, Neil, builder at Lagnagarach. Alexander – a private in the 1st Argyll Rifle Volunteers – was accorded a tumultuous public reception on his return to Campbeltown. His awards included £250 – a huge sum at that time – and a gold badge worth £50. The Wimbledon coal-pit, sunk to the west of Drumlemble in 1881, was named in celebration of his marksmanship.[53]

Ferguson families occurred in many parts of Scotland, Highland and Lowland. The name appears in Kintyre in the late seventeenth century, e.g. Neil fergusone in Barr, 1692, and Hugh fferguson in Craigs, 1695.[54] In the nineteenth and twentieth centuries, the name was extensive in the Southend farming community. Andrew McKerral attributes the presence of the name in south Kintyre to Lowland plantation,[55] but there were certainly, in Kintyre as a whole, Gaelic Fergusons (*Mac Fhearghais*), and they appear as 'McFergish' and 'McKerras' in early records.

19. BLACK. This badly eroding sandstone monument commemorates Duncan Black, fisherman, and his wife Margaret Vetters (died 1916). Duncan was a son of Daniel Black, fisherman – born c 1833, of parents from Rathlin Island – and his first wife, Margaret Morrison, whose father, John, was also from Rathlin. The Black family settled in Campbeltown c. 1838, intermarried extensively and became prominent in the local fishing community. The name probably represents *Mac Ghille Dhuibh*, Son of the Black Lad, from Scottish migration.[56] Incidentally, the descendants of the 'fishing Blacks' have been notable, generation after generation, for fine singing voices, which might suggest a connection with the internationally acclaimed Irish singing sisters, Mary and Frances Black, whose father belonged to Rathlin.

The surname Vetters looks like a true exotic. I've heard it said that the progenitor of the family was a Napoleonic War prisoner who settled in Campbeltown after his liberation, but the truth probably lies closer to home. Vetters appears to be yet another native surname in disguise: from 'McPheder' or 'Pheder', Gaelic *Mac Pheadair*, 'Son of Peter', which apparently also produced McFater, earlier 'McIlepheddir' (Gaelic *Mac Gille Pheadair*, Son of the Devotee of Saint Peter), and the sole surviving form, Paterson. The parents of Margaret, above, were Christopher Vetters, fisherman, and Mary McPhee. The rather genteel forename 'Christopher' can be traced back at least as far as Christopher Vetters, military pensioner, whose son Dugald died in 1875. The peculiar female Christian name, Montgomery, recurs in the Vetters family and appears on this stone. See Appendix for further discussion of unusual forenames. George F. Black, in his monumental *The Surnames of Scotland* (1946), surely could not have missed out many names, but 'Vetters' was one that he did miss. It survives into the twenty-first century as the middle name of a lady who lives near Campbeltown, and 'Loynachan' (no. 42) too survives, as the middle name of a Campbeltown lady.

20. MACKINVEN. James McKinven and his wife Christina Keith, commemorated here, produced two sons who are locally remembered – if tenuously now – as minor poets. The poems of Angus Keith MacKinven and Donald MacKinven were preserved by their mother and published, posthumously and privately, in a booklet titled *A Few Original Poems and Other Writings*.

Both brothers emigrated to Canada. Donald, the younger, died of typhoid fever on 23/2/1907, aged 19, just 11 months after arriving in Canada. Angus died, on 12/10/1916, at the age of 30, in Rouen*, of wounds received in the Battle of the Somme while serving with the 19th Alberta Dragoons Divisional Cavalry. Angus used two pen-names, 'Ceann Loch gu Brath' (Gaelic, 'Campbeltown Forever') and 'A K Love', which latter was explained thus in the booklet: 'The surname Love is derived from "MacIonmhuinn", the Gaelic for MacKinven, and meaning "The son of Love".'

Love certainly was in use in Kintyre as an anglicisation of MacKinven, but MacKinven itself, as a surname, is of dubious validity and is likely to be a variant of MacKinnon. Indeed, in the eighteenth and nineteenth century records, the two names sometimes occur in the same family or even attached to the same individual, e.g.

---

*The particulars inscribed on the gravestone are curiously at variance with those given in the biographical notes contained in the booklet of poems, here cited for comparison.

'John MacKinnon or MacKinvin,' shoemaker in Campbeltown in 1791. In the opinion of the late Rev William Matheson, an expert on Highland genealogy, *Mac Ionmhuinn* (MacKinven) derives from *Mac Fhionnghuin* (MacKinnon): 'There was no such surname as *Mac Ionmhuinn*, except in the minds of those who spelt it that way or accepted the spelling. In pronunciation, the difference is so slight as to make the folk etymology plausible.'[57]

Curiously, the names Love and MacKinnon were conjoined in the marriage of Peter MacKinnon of Ronachan and Rosemount – a nephew of Sir William MacKinnon – and Jane Love, a daughter of Alexander Love, merchant, and Helen MacNaughton.[58] They are buried in the hollow in Section 1.

Gregor Robertson, grandson of the late Provost Dan McKinven of Campbeltown and Beth McMillan of Carradale, is a professional footballer and has been capped for the Scotland Under-21s. His mother is the elder of the two McKinven sisters, Mhairi, and his father the political activist Robbie the Pict.

21. RALSTON. Against the wall, five stones to the south of No. 20, this memorial to Gavin Ralston (1823–1911), farmer in Kilmichael, and his wife Martha Young. Gavin's first wife, Jessie Dunlop, whom he married in Southend on 5/4/1855, died young, leaving two daughters. From Gavin and his second wife, therefore, descend all the Ralstons at present in Kintyre. In other words, had Gavin never remarried or had Martha Young failed to produce sons, the Ralston name would have disappeared here. Such is the tenuousness by which some surnames have endured, while others – once numerous – have disappeared (not least through emigration). Three generations on from Gavin in Kilmichael, the various branches of the Ralston family successfully farm extensive lands in Kintyre.

The Ralston farming tradition itself appears to have been maintained against the odds, because Gavin was first apprenticed as a shoemaker, then successively engaged in the draff trade in Campbeltown, started a flesher's business and opened a dairy, before 'his father's occupation claimed him and held him'. His first farm was Gallowhill, where he spent 21 years. He then took the lease of Kilmichael, but disaster struck shortly after his move there. His entire herd of Ayrshire cattle was wiped out by rinderpest, a virulent infectious disease. There was no compensation available at that time, but by sheer determination he soon renewed his stock and continued in Kilmichael until his death.[59]

Gavin's birthplace, Gartloskin, is recorded on the stone. The name – from Gaelic *Gart Losgainn*, Toad Field – survives attached to the afforested hill at the back of Dalbuie, but there were once two farms there, High and Low Gartloskin. Also descended from that Gartloskin branch was Dr Gavin 'Guy' Ralston, MA, LLB, MB, ChB, FRCSE, FRCSG (1912–2003), a distinguished surgeon and occasional contributor to *The Kintyre Magazine*. His final article – an evocative and impeccably crafted memoir of his early childhood on Macharioch Farm, Southend – appeared in issue no. 54, shortly before his death.

In 2004, I corresponded with, and finally met, another descendant of Gartloskin Ralstons, Robert 'Bob' Ralston, a dental surgeon in Leicester. His great-great-great grandfather, Gavin, who married Margaret Wilson, got the lease of High Gartloskin in 1771, when he was described as 'tenant in Knockstaplebeg', a nearby farm. Bob's great-grandfather, Gavin Ralston, was born at Gartloskin about 1803, married Agnes Mitchell and afterwards moved to Coatbridge, Lanarkshire, where Bob himself was born. Knowledge of the family connection with Kintyre had persisted down to Bob's generation, but it was vague. When Bob's great-grandfather's parents – Robert Ralston, farmer, and Janet Wallace (of Machribeg) – were finally identified in Robert's death certificate, the Gartloskin connection at once became apparent. Robert and his wife, Iris, visited Kintyre in September 2004, and were able to meet not only many of his Ralston kin, but also several Wallace relatives. That characteristic Ralston forename, Gavin, has been preserved in Bob's family to the present time – his eldest son, a doctor in Birmingham, is Gavin.

As with many of the prominent Lowland plantation families in south Kintyre, the history of the Ralston family has been minutely researched for publication. Andrew McKerral's account of William Ralston of Ralston, 'the living head of an ancient Scottish family', in *Kintyre in the Seventeenth Century*, pp 87–89, is a useful introduction, as is Guy Ralston's more detailed 'William Ralston of That Ilk' in *The Kintyre Magazine*, No. 8.

William, who died at the age of 81 in 1691 – towards the close of what was arguably the most anarchic century in Scotland's history – is buried in Kilcolmkill, Southend, his coat of arms inscribed in the stone and his body facing north instead of the customary south. As Guy Ralston remarks at the close of his account: 'Some say that it was his wish that he should lie facing his farm of Keil; others that he wished to ensure that his back was towards Rome.'

Martha Young, above, belonged to another Lowland family in Kintyre, but one which arrived much later, in the latter half of the nineteenth century, from Gartcosh in the Parish of Beith, Ayrshire, where she was born c. 1834.[60]

The universal tendency among Lowland Plantation families in south Kintyre to marry exclusively within their own stock persisted until about 1820, after which some marriages into 'Highland' families begin to be recorded. The division between the two groups, which shared the same living conditions on the land, was essentially linguistic: Scots on the one side and Gaelic on the other.

Division 5

22. MCFADYEN. This simple painted wooden memorial, recently erected against the wall, and its inscription already fading, marks the grave of Marjorie McFadyen, who died, on 26/5/1981, at the age of 104, and who must therefore be one of oldest persons interred here, if not the oldest. She was born on 8 August 1876 in Campbeltown and was one of the first pupils to attend St Kieran's RC School, of which she was later pupil-teacher, assistant teacher and finally head teacher. In the final years of her life, failing sight forced her to enter the Cottage Hospital, whence she went to Witchburn Hospital, where she died.

Remarkably, one of those who attended her 102nd birthday celebration was a retired Campbeltown fisherman, John McWhirter, who had been a pupil of hers and was himself 92 years old! He remembered her catching him by the ear, on his first day at school, and asking him, 'And who are you?' She was just 15 then and her red hair reached almost to her thighs.[61]

Her father was Henry McFadyen, seaman and fisherman, born about 1839 in Derry, Ireland. In Campbeltown, he married first Jane Black (in 1862) – but she must have died several years afterwards – and then Mary O'Hara (in 1872).[62]

The nineteenth century progenitor of the McFadyen family of

building and haulage contractors in Campbeltown was a shepherd, John McFadyen, from Torosay Parish, Isle of Mull.

23. GRUMOLI. This stone commemorates Leonello Grumoli (died 28/2/1972, aged 86), his wife Maria Moscardini (died 2/6/1968, aged 81) and three of their children, who belonged to the small community of café-owning Italians which settled in Campbeltown in the early twentieth century. Leo and Maria came in 1911, with one child – Emma, born in Italy – having purchased a café in Kirk Street. Business being good, Leo sent for his young brother Umberto ('Bertie') Grumoli (1893–1957) and his wife Claudina Santi (1895–1959).

The Grumoli brothers were born and brought up at Renaio, a small village in the Tuscan hills above Barga. Maria Moscardini was from the nearby village of Carpinecchio. Maria's brother, Gioni – or 'Johnny' – Moscardini is still remembered in Campbeltown for his footballing skills. He was an Italian internationalist – nine appearances and seven goals – and played for Campbeltown Former Pupils Amateur Football Club during a brief residence in Campbeltown in the mid-1920s.

Leo and Maria had seven more children, all born in Campbeltown:

Alf, Neli, Robert, Geni, Lidia, Italo and Dora. Umberto and Claudina had five children: Yole, Oswald, Renato, Maria, and Robina, the last of whom died young. The family owned the Mayfair, Locarno and Royal cafés, popularly referred to as the 'Top', 'Middle' and 'Bottom'. Ironically, while the Grumoli offspring were one by one 'called up' during the Second World War – 24-year-old Italo lost his life at Arnhem in 1944 – the fathers were interned as aliens of enemy nationality and the mothers obliged to leave Campbeltown!

The other local Italian name, Togneri, stems from the marriage of Jack Togneri to Emma Grumoli in 1938.[63]

24. GULLIVER. Here, buried with his parents – William Frederick Gulliver (1892–1977) and Mary Martha Lafferty (1892–1975) – lies James Gerald Gulliver (1930–96), the multimillionaire business genius who 'transformed the face of British food retailing in Scotland . . .'[64] and who was described in 1987 as 'amongst the most successful businessmen Britain has ever produced'.[65]

A grocer's son, he was educated at Campbeltown Grammar School, whence, with a scholarship, he went to the University of Glasgow and earned a first in engineering. After graduation, he studied for a year at the Georgia Institute of Technology in the US (not at Harvard Business School, as he once claimed, somewhat to his discredit). In 1982, after various astute business ventures – he had received, 10 years earlier, *The Guardian* Young Businessman of the Year award – Gulliver bought the Allied Suppliers grocery chains from Sir James Goldsmith, bringing him Presto and Templetons in Scotland, which he then merged with his Allied Distilled Products off-licence company to create Argyll Foods.

By 1985, Argyll Foods had an annual turnover approaching £1800m and profits exceeding £50m; but in December of that year, Gulliver, backed by the Royal Bank of Scotland, formally launched a bid for Distillers Co Ltd. – ultimately and controversially thwarted by Guinness – and set in motion 'an episode which is one of the darkest in the annals of the City', and which culminated, in 1990, after years of protracted legal proceedings and trials, in the jailing of Ernest Saunders, formerly chairman of Guinness, and two other City figures.

By purchasing Safeway and merging it with Argyll, Gulliver

created one of the biggest supermarket chains in Britain; but in 1988 he resigned and failed thereafter to repeat his earlier successes. He was married four times and his interests included two farms in Fife, properties in London, Manchester and Cheltenham, and a 'small but splendid fleet of cars'.[66]

Gulliver was of Irish stock on his mother's side. His grandfather, Edward Lafferty, a carter from west Donegal, married, on 9/6/1887, Mary McKay, whose parents, Denis McKay, fisherman, and Margaret McKendrick, came to Campbeltown from Red Bay on the Antrim coast.

Division 3

25. McLEAN. This stone – set against the south-facing wall, but now practically obscured by an evergreen bush – commemorates, among other family members, James McLean, who was killed during the disastrous Dardanelles campaign of 1915. This military effort – launched to divert pressure from Russian forces in the Caucasus – began, on 18 March, with an exclusively Naval operation, which failed to force the Narrows. Thereafter, a hastily assembled force, under the command of General Sir Ian Hamilton, was tasked with seizing the Gallipoli Peninsula, but two major offensives were successfully resisted by the Turkish defenders and withdrawal of Allied forces was completed in January, 1916.[67]

`Corporal McLean, of the 4th Argyll Mountain Battery, was killed near Krithia on 12/7/1915, at the age of 22. His gun – one of two which were 'out forward of the Battery' – had seen regular action over a six-week period, but, on that 'black day' in July, the Turks decided to '"search around" with high explosive and shrapnel bullets', and found that Argyll gun. Another Campbeltown gunner, Corporal Archibald Johnston, was among the four killed.[68] James McLean is buried in Twelve Trees Copse Cemetery, which is near Krithia and contains the graves of 3,266 British and Commonwealth dead, of which 1,953 were unidentified.[69]

The 4th Argyll Mountain Battery, which landed at Gallipoli on 30 April, was until 1908 known as the 6th Argyllshire Artillery Volunteers, based first at Kilkerran and afterwards at New Orleans, where the windowless magazine still stands and the concrete remains of the gun-mountings can still be found in the grass.[70] The Territorial Army Hall, demolished early in 2004, was built in 1871 as the drill hall of the Artillery Volunteers.[71] On the War Memorial, Campbeltown, the Argyll Mountain Battery is represented by 15 names.

James McLean's father, Neil – died 16/11/1938, aged 81 – was a well-known and successful herring fisherman. When the family's first modern ring-netter was built in 1932, she was named the *Margaret Hamilton* after Neil's wife, who died 29/1/1943, aged 79. Neil was a son of Joseph 'Josie' McLean (died 1880), who in 1832, at the age of 13, joined the Campbeltown & Glasgow Steam Packet Company as an apprentice on board the *Duke of Lancaster*. One of his duties was to 'go through the town at night or morning, as the case might be, blowing his foghorn . . . to apprise passengers of the hour of departure'.[72]

As a surname in Kintyre, MacLean – Gaelic *Mac Ghill Eathain*, Son of the Devotee of Saint John, among several variants – does not appear in real strength until the eighteenth century. In the Work Horse Tax lists of 1797,[73] nine MacLean farmers are recorded, including, in south Kintyre, John in Ronochan, John in lower Darlochan, Andrew and Alexander in Kilmahone (Kilmaho), Duncan in Calliburn and Donald in Gartgrulin. Many of the numerous MacLean families in nineteenth century Campbeltown Parish were drawn from a wide geographical area, including Ireland and Skye.

Joseph McLean's wife was Jean McKinlay, born in March, 1819, at 'Corribeg' according to the Old Parish Registers, and at 'Knockscalbert' according to the Register of Poor;[74] so presumably 'Corribeg' was a habitation, hitherto unrecorded and now unknown, on Knockscalbert, the hill to the north of Campbeltown. Certainly, her parents were in that area when they married on 15 June, 1813: Neil McKinlay, weaver, was of Skeroblin, and Barbara McGill was a daughter of Neil McGill, farmer, Calliburn.

There have been MacKinlays – Gaelic *Mac Fhionnlaigh*, Son of Finlay – in Kintyre since at least the late seventeenth century: Lauchlan in Kilmichael, Carradale, in 1685, and 'ffinlay' in Campbeltown, 1692. In the nineteenth and twentieth centuries, the name was most closely associated with the fishing community at Dalintober. Peter McKinlay CBE, a fisherman's son, born in Campbeltown in 1939, has had a distinguished career in the Scottish Office and beyond – e.g. Director, Scottish Prison Service (1988–91), Chief Executive, Scottish Homes (1991–99) – for further particulars of which see the current *Who's Who* or *Who's Who in Scotland*.

26. HUGHES. The main stone here – 'ERECTED BY THE DAUGHTERS' (Elizabeth and Isabella Hughes) – is rather enigmatic and certainly requires more explanation than most. First, the persons it commemorates are not actually named, though the surname does appear at the base of the inscription. Second, the drowning alluded to was not an isolated accident: the entire crew of a Campbeltown fishing-skiff drowned on 22 December, 1909. Unusually, though, a second, smaller stone has been erected in front of the main stone to remedy the omission of the parents' names.

James 'Jimmy' Hughes was skipper of Archie Cook Sr's *Victor* and had been fishing in Kilbrannan Sound that day. About noon the wind began to rise and weather signs were ominous. Most of the fleet headed at once for harbour, but Jimmy lingered awhile, hoping, no doubt, to gather a few more fish. A bitterly cold south-easterly blew up, bringing heavy seas and sleet and snow showers in the night.

On the following morning, Robert McCaig, Ardnacross, was walking on the shore there and noticed a mass of driftwood lying near the mouth of the burn. There was a dead man – Duncan McSporran – lying close by and, on the Gull Rock offshore, could be seen 'the top of a mast . . . sticking out of the water'. McCaig walked to town and reported his grim discovery. By then, two Peninver fishermen, Robert Cameron and John McMillan, had found the body of Jimmy Hughes, 'fully dressed' in sea-boots, oilskins and sou'wester. McSporran, who was a 'powerful swimmer', had, on the contrary, removed his oilskins and boots, and obviously struck out for the shore.

The entire crew of five perished: Hughes (41), Bolgam Street, married with eight children; Duncan Campbell (60), Corbett's Close, married without children; Duncan McSporran (26), Fisher Row, married with three children; John McIntyre (27), Dalaruan, married with one child, and Robert McMillan (16), son of Robert McMillan, fisherman, Broombrae, 'and recently of Ballochantee'.[75]

James Hughes's wife, Isabella, was registered on the 'Poor Roll' of Campbeltown Parish on 24 January, 1910, and awarded 6s a week. Her four eldest children were already working, but the remainder were either at school or at home. Isabella was herself Hughes by name, born in Greenock on 11/5/1871, daughter of Richard Hughes, quarryman, and Elizabeth McMaster.[76]

Richard Hughes himself was earlier a recipient of Poor Relief. In August, 1889, at the age of 48, he was brought from Kilkivan Quarry to Campbeltown and admitted to the Poor House with his left arm and both legs fractured after a fall from the face of the quarry. He was born in Londonderry, but had been in Scotland 'since infancy', and his wife, Elizabeth, was from County Down.[77]

27. MCBAIN. This is not really a local name, though it was recorded in Kintyre in the seventeenth century. Robert McBain (died 13/4/1949, aged 84) and Martha Galbraith (died 31/7/1939, aged 72) were the parents of Neil McBain, the most successful footballer Campbeltown has yet produced, though since his father was an 'incomer' and his mother apparently from Carradale, it's a question of whether genes or geography was the more decisive influence.

He played locally for the Academicals, signed for Ayr United in 1918, then moved to England, playing, as a centre-half, first for Manchester United and then for Everton. He was capped thrice for Scotland in full internationals: 1922, in a team which beat England

1–0 at Villa Park, Birmingham; 1923, against Northern Ireland at Windsor Park, Belfast, when Scotland again won 1–0; 1924, against Wales, which beat Scotland 2–0 at Ninian Park, Cardiff. In all three games, he shared Scotland's colours with the legendary 'Wee Blue Devil', Alan Morton of Rangers.[78]

McBain also has the distinction – unlikely to be surpassed – of being the oldest player ever to appear in a senior professional football match in Britain, when, on 15 March, 1947, at the age of 52, he turned out in goal, against Hartlepool United, for the club he then managed, New Brighton, both his registered goalkeepers being injured at the time.[79]

Robert and Martha McBain married on 31 December 1884, had six sons and six daughters and celebrated their golden wedding anniversary at Kinloch Place in 1934.[80]

28. TOWNSLEY, BOSWELL. This stone commemorates a husband and wife of the 'Tinker', or Traveller, community, William Townsley (died 7/5/1981) and Elizabeth Boswell (died 19/11/1956). Though other Traveller graves can be found throughout the cemetery – MacPhee and Williamson were the other main families associated with Kintyre – this one is of particular interest on account of the Boswell name, which is clearly Romany, though intermarriage between Romanies and Scottish Travellers was very unusual. Yet, the two groups share a similar background. The Romanies, or 'Gypsies', are believed to have originated as metal-workers in north-west India, arriving in Europe in the fifteenth and sixteenth centuries AD.

The Scottish Tinkers were also, as the name implies, originally metal-workers, though latterly, as well as making and mending tin utensils, they wove and sold willow baskets, told fortunes, hired themselves as seasonal farm-workers, gathered rags and scrap metal, and hawked clothes-pegs etc. round the countryside. Throughout Kintyre, there are dozens of sites where Traveller families once pitched their tents, but these have entirely fallen into disuse and the remnants of the Traveller families, forced off the roads by increasing motor traffic and bureaucratic restrictions, have been housed.

'Travellers', in their various groupings, have for centuries been widely despised and persecuted; consequently, they preferred to keep to themselves and to communicate by private language. Ironically,

Boswell
Tinker woman and child at her tent door

TOWNSLEY/BOSWELL.

however, as the disintegration of that insular Traveller culture accelerated in the latter half of the twentieth century, ethnologists engaged in recording tradition-bearers among its scattered communities discovered an immense and hitherto unsuspected wealth of story and song.

For an 'inside' understanding of that vanishing culture, the late Betsy Whyte's marvellous autobiographies, *The Yellow on the Broom* (1979) and *Red Rowans and Wild Honey* (1990), are essential reading. Betsy was herself a Townsley, as was the mother (born in the cave at Ballachgoichan, Muasdale) of Duncan Williamson, who is now the best-known of the Scottish Travellers, through his public story-telling and books. His autobiography, *The Horsie Man* (1994), may be recommended.[81]

In former times, Travellers might be buried in some remote spot, interred as they were born – unregistered. In a roadside oak copse near Oragaig, in north Kintyre, a Traveller baby was buried under a tree, to which was later attached a small plaque recording 'Baby Hestia – Registered.'[82] The name must be an extreme rarity: Hestia, in Greek mythology, became a household deity of the hearth and fire. And by fire were consumed the tents and caravans and the personal belongings – valuables, such as jewellery excepted – of Travellers who had died. Moreover, a family's quarrelling over the possessions of a dead relative was utterly incomprehensible to Tinkers and Romanies alike.

The funeral of Bella Townsley – 'self-styled Queen of the Kintyre Tinkers' – was observed by groups of townsfolk gathered along the route to Kilkerran Cemetery. Popularly known as 'Bonny Bella', from her lovely blonde hair and fair complexion, she was born Isabella Williamson in Tangy Glen and was 55 years old when she died on 23 April 1949. The cortège was led by a nephew, Alexander Townsley, playing 'Lochaber No More' and 'The Flowers of the Forest' on his bagpipes. 'As the tinkers have not much work on the farms just now they could not afford to perform their customary rite of throwing silver coins into the grave. They believe that this act keeps bad luck away from the remainder of the family.'[83]

29. ROBERTSON. Robert Robertson (died 20/1/1940, aged 59), commemorated here with his wife Mary Bell and later family members, unquestionably ranks as the most innovative and influential Campbeltown fisherman of the twentieth century. In 1907, he was the first on the West Coast of Scotland to instal motor power on a fishing vessel, the skiff *Brothers,* and in 1922 he ventured on an even greater gamble with the launch of a radical new design of ring-netter from the boat-yard of James Miller & Sons, St Monans. The

'ROBERTSON' Robert Robertson
'The Hoodie' – innovative fisherman.

Falcon and *Frigate Bird* constituted a singular departure from the traditional Loch Fyne Skiff: they were bigger, canoe-sterned and completely decked, with a wheel-house at the stern.

Success did not come at once to Robertson and his partners, but within several years his model was adopted more widely and eventually became the standard herring ring-netter throughout the British Isles. Unusually, Robertson had travelled extensively in the study of fishing boats and methods – to Norway, the USA and Australia, where he briefly settled – but in his final years he was afflicted by blindness, which forced him into early retirement. He had an extraordinary hunters' instinct for being in the right place at the right time, a gift possessed by only the greatest of fishermen. His nick-name was 'The Hoodie', after the film character 'The Hooded Terror'.[84]

Robertson's rather confused family background was not untypical of the period and included the almost obligatory infusion of Irish blood. His great-grandfather, James Robertson, was a soldier whose wife, Judy Devine, gave birth to a son, Robert, 'at sea between

Britain and Gibraltar'. That son was The Hoodie's grandfather, who married Catherine McCann and earned his living as a hawker. Robert and Catherine had three children, Hugh, Susan and Patrick, all born in Govan. On 27/10/1879, Hugh married Mary Mathieson, a daughter of Dugald Mathieson who was drowned at the age of 31 when the *Mystery* was wrecked at Machrihanish (no. 1). Mary's mother, Helen McDougall, married again, in 1871, to another fisherman, William McLellan. Hugh Robertson and Mary Mathieson had three children, Robert (born 1880), Mary (born 1882) and Hughina, born a month after her father was lost with the schooner *Moy* (no. 2). Hugh's widow also married again, in 1887, to a prominent Campbeltown fisherman, John 'The Junk' McIntyre, and it was within that family that Robert Robertson was reared.[85]

These Robertsons no longer survive by name in Kintyre. The other – extensive – Robertson fishing family descends from James Robertson – born 6/2/1781 – and his wife Marion Agnew, who are in Kilchousland, the traditional burial-ground of the Dalintober population.

30. CLIFFORD. This stone commemorates the esteemed Scottish architect, Henry E Clifford (died 14/10/1932, aged 80) and his wife

·CLIFFORD.   Grangeard by Henry E. Clifford.

Margaret Alice Gibson (died 29/07/1933, aged 57). Clifford had a double connection with Campbeltown: his mother, Rebecca Anderson, belonged here, as did his wife, who was a daughter of Dr William Gibson (1824–1922). As Katherine McNeil remarks of Clifford, 'A measure of the quality of his work is evident in that he was one of the Scottish architects noted in the contemporary publication *Das Englische Haus*, and the only Glaswegian architect, along with Charles Rennie Mackintosh (1868–1928), to have a project featured.'[86]

At the age of 15, in 1867, Clifford was apprenticed to the practice of eminent Glasgow architect, John Burnet Sr. In 1878, he established his own practice, the first important project for which was Craigard, Low Askomil, designed in 1882 for local distiller, William McKersie. Successive projects in Campbeltown include Auchinlee and Bellfield (1884); St Kiaran's Episcopal Church Rectory (1885–86); the Christian Institute (1885); the original Victoria Hall and the Mission Church Hall, Kinloch Road (1888); The Club and Redholme (1896); Redcliff (1897) and Norwood (1898). He was also architect to Campbeltown School Board.[87]

31. CAMPBELL. Five gravestones to members of the Campbell family of Kildalloig, who later succeeded to the Baronetcy of Auchinbreck, stand within an iron-railed enclosure, that to Sir Charles Ralph Campbell, 11th Baronet of Auchinbreck (in Cowal), being the plainest to read. That distinguished family descended from Sir Duncan Campbell of Lochow, by his second wife, Margaret Stewart, daughter of Sir John Stewart of Blackhall, natural son of King Robert III. This account, however, will concentrate first on an earlier member of the Auchinbreck family, Sir Duncan Campbell, and his harrowing death during the Civil War which ravaged much of Argyll in the mid-seventeenth century.

Sir Duncan – 'the darling of the women of Kintyre', and 'a stout soldier, but vicious man' – was in command of the Covenanting army which his chief, Archibald Campbell, Marquess of Argyll, assembled for a punitive strike against the Royalist force, commanded by James Graham, Marquess of Montrose, following the sacking of Campbell lands in Argyll and the burning of Inveraray. The Covenanting force, 3000-strong, marched north, but was surprised by the Royalists at Inverlochy, on 2 February 1645, and suffered unprecedented – indeed, incomprehensible – slaughter, rout and humiliation. Sir Duncan, according to tradition, had fought bravely, but was finally captured and taken to Montrose's second-in-command, Alasdair MacColla, who would offer him only a choice of deaths: hanging or decapitation. In a phrase which subsequently became proverbial, the helpless general replied: *Dà dhiù gun aon roghainn* ('Two evils and no choice'), whereupon MacColla hacked at his head and killed him.[88]

This Alasdair MacColla – more formally, Major-General Sir Alexander MacDonald, as he became – was a powerful giant of a man. A son of Coll MacDonald of Colonsay, his martial feats became legendary in Gaelic tradition. In 1644, his kinsman, Randall MacDonald, Earl of Antrim, commissioned him to lead an army into Scotland in support of the Royalist cause, and in August of that year he linked up with Montrose. Within a year, they had defeated the Covenanters in six battles. MacColla's primary motive, in all of this, was to wreak destruction on the detested Campbells and to recover the forfeit Clan Donald lands, Kintyre among them.

By 1647, however, time was running out for Alasdair MacColla, because a force of battle-seasoned Covenanters, commanded by General David Leslie, was hastening north from England. It caught up with MacColla – by then parted from Montrose – at Rhunahaorine, where MacColla and a part of his army escaped to Islay in boats, while the remainder continued south, under the command of Archibald Mor MacDonald of Sanda. They went as far south as they could, which was Dunaverty Castle, and there awaited their fate.

It was to be a hard fate. Leslie and his army laid siege to the Castle and immediately cut off its water-supply. When the garrison surrendered, a few days later – at the beginning of June – it was massacred with few exceptions. Most of the estimated 300 men who had been holed up in the tiny castle were from Kintyre and other parts of Argyll.

Ranald, the young grandson of Archibald Mor MacDonald, was, according to local tradition, smuggled to safety by his nurse, Flora MacCambridge. The infant's father, Lieutenant Colonel Archibald Og MacDonald, was killed later that year in the Battle of Knocknanuss in Munster, Ireland, along with Alasdair MacColla himself, who appears to have been captured and executed without trial.

MacColla's family connections with Kintyre were extensive: two of his sisters married into prominent Kintyre families – the MacKays of Ardnacross and the MacDonalds of Largie – MacColla himself married into one of the greatest of Kintyre families, the MacAllisters of Loup, descended from Alasdair Mor, a great-grandson of Somerled, Lord of the Isles; and his mother, Mary, was a daughter of Ranald MacDonald of Smerby.[89]

Mary was also a second cousin of Coll Ciotach, her husband, as a result of which marriage the present chief of Clan Donald South (*Clann MacIain Mhóir*), Count Randal MacDonnell, represents both the senior male line of the family and the senior female line of descent from the first chief, Iain Mhóir.[90]

Golden-haired Mary Campbell, Robert Burns's 'Highland Mary', whom he pledged to marry, was brought up at Broombrae, Saddell Street, and attended school in a nearby thatched house. She was born in 1766 on a farm near Dunoon, but came to Campbeltown as an infant when her father, Archibald, found employment as a seaman in the Revenue service (no. 3). She died on 17 October, 1786, at Greenock.

32. MACKAY. Donald MacKay was born in 1836 on the now afforested farm of Erradil, between Feochaig and Glenehervie, on the southern Learside. After his schooling, he was apprenticed to a firm of Glasgow carpenters, but returned to Kintyre and entered into business with Archibald MacQueen, boat-builder in Campbeltown, who is interred nearby. In 1877, he became a partner in the Campbeltown Shipbuilding Company, an ambitious project – established on Trench Point – which, by the time of its closure in 1922, had built 116 iron vessels, of 151,000 gross tonnage.

An elder of Lorne Street Free Church and, by political persuasion, a 'Liberal-Unionist', he was also 'interested in all philanthropic and benevolent institutions and objects' and 'a prominent advocate of temperance'. He died suddenly of heart failure at his home, Greystone Cottage, High Askomil, on 22/12/1899, leaving his wife, Amelia Morrison Fraser, five sons and a daughter.[91] In the year after his death, his estate was valued at £31,267 17s 6d, a considerable sum at the time.

His parents were Peter MacKay and Janet MacKerral of Brunerican, who belonged to another, and longer established,

44

·MACKAY·

Peter MacKay - designer of MacKay's Patent Hay-Rick Lifter.

Southend family. The marriage of Peter and Janet produced a rather distinguished crop of males.

Peter, who followed Donald, was born at Erradil in 1839. He was in business in Campbeltown as a coachbuilder and wheelwright, but is best remembered for having designed MacKay's Patent Hay-Rick Lifter, which he marketed throughout the British Isles. Curiously, he and his wife, Margaret Lightbody, died within 10 hours of each other on 9 July 1914.

Archibald was the last MacKay born at Erradil, in 1841, and the only son who continued the farming tradition. In 1878 he took the tenancy of Lephenstrath, and many descendants of his marriage to Mary McDonald are still farming in Southend, though the name MacKay itself has disappeared.

Godfrey, born in 1845 at Knockstapplemore, became a draughtsman in Greenock. Neil, also born in Knockstapplemore, in 1851, attended the University of Glasgow, whence he graduated MA in 1875 and BD in 1878. He was minister in Ochiltree, in the Presbytery of Ayr, from 1880, and died there in 1930.

The first MacKays in Erradil were Archibald and his sons Donald and Neil, who got the tenancy in 1797, having previously been in Aros. Family tradition maintains a descent from the MacKay of Ugadale – variously identified as Ivor or his son Gille-Crist – who helped the fugitive Robert Bruce cross Kintyre in 1306 (Gille-Crist's land-holdings in Kintyre were confirmed by crown charter in 1329). The claim is impossible to prove; it is also, by the same token, impossible to disprove! The evidence is assessed in an account of mine published in *The Kintyre Magazine*, No. 40, pp 27–29, from which the preceding biographical summaries of Donald MacKay's brothers are extracted.

MacKay – Gaelic *Mac Aiodh* – is one of the oldest families in Kintyre and represents a surname which stabilised earlier than most, for until the sixteenth century many surnames were of the patronymic type, i.e. the child's surname taken from the father's forename, and mutating generation by generation.

The Kintyre MacKays have no connection with the principal family of Strathnaver, but are of the same family as the MacGees in Ulster and the MacGhies in Galloway.[92]

One of the two medieval cross-shafts in Kilkerran was dedicated to Cristinus MacKay and his unnamed wife. He is believed to have been a MacKay of Ugadale, in which the name *Gille-Crist*, Devotee of Christ – represented here by 'Cristinus' – recurs,[93] and on which the surname, in general terms, Gilchrist is based.

Nineteenth century Irish immigration brought into South Kintyre several MacKay families from County Antrim. Some later figured prominently in the Campbeltown fishing industry and intermarried extensively in the local Catholic population; but these MacKays had likely fled from Kintyre to Ireland during the disintegration of Clan Donald in Argyll, and so, in a sense, were merely returning home.[94]

33. TODD. Two gravestones – the east-facing one to Archibald, who died in his 89th year at Strone, Southend, on 2/7/1923, and the west-facing one to George of Gartgunnal, Tangy, who died 6/5/1938, aged 91 – represent a now locally extinct Borders shepherding family.

Their father was George Todd, who arrived in Kintyre in 1844 as shepherd at Allt an Tairbh (merged by then with Stramollach and Mulbuy). The Todds originated in Dumfriesshire, but were hardly typical of the other nineteenth century Borders shepherding families in Kintyre, Beattie, Borthwick, Helm and Jackson. An intermediate settlement in Mid-Argyll turned the Todd family into Gaelic speakers, and when, in the late 1930s and early '40s, the Scandinavian linguist, Nils M Holmer, was conducting his Gaelic research – published in 1972 as *The Gaelic of Kintyre* – three of his six informants in Southend were the Strone-born siblings Jessie Todd, at Balnamoil, and George and Katie Todd at Tangy.[95] The name comes from *tod*, a fox in Scots and Northern English dialect.

34. MCSPORRAN. There are many McSporrans buried in Kilkerran, but I have selected James McSporran (died 2/6/1920, aged 73), first because the farm he tenanted, Strabane, has, like him, disappeared – it was absorbed into HMS Landrail, the naval airfield at Machrihanish commissioned in 1941 – and, second, because his wife, Jean Blue, also bore an old and interesting surname.

For anyone who has grown up in Kintyre, McSporran is just another name, and a common one at that; but, to a stranger to the place and its people, the reaction to the name might be incredulity or downright derision. To some of our Southern neighbours it sounds as though it should be attached to some stage Scot with drooping kilt and outrageously feathered balmoral.

Here is an apposite sample from a mid-twentieth century booklet of 'humorous Scottish Stories', *"Tell Me Another!"*: 'INELIGIBLE! Mrs MacSporran (reading from paper) "Burns was a Scotsman, but

a citizen of the world. He was an internationalist." Mr MacSporran: "Awa' wi ye, wumman. There wis nae fitba in his day."[96]

The late Duncan McSporran, a Dalintober fisherman, once told me that in Whitby, Yorkshire, he was refused the facility of wiring money home to his wife because the postal clerkess refused to believe his name. He had to return to the boat and obtain documentary proof of his identity. More recently, on 7 October, 1995, Iain Archibald McSporran, Drumlemble, won a SKY TV 'phone in' sports competition. The presenter, reading from a card, admitted that, in brackets next to Iain's name, the assurance, 'NOT A WIND-UP', had been appended.

Campbeltown's connection with the internationally renowned mountaineer Dougal Haston (1940–77) is at once evident in his full name, Duncan Curdy McSporran Haston, which encapsulates the marriage (5/3/1876) in Campbeltown of Archibald McSporran and Margaret Curdie, daughter of Charles Curdie and Catherine McKay.

Haston, who was born in Currie, Midlothian, and died in a ski-ing accident in the Rhone Valley, Switzerland, was the first Briton to climb the north face of the Eiger (1960) and prominent in the first ascent of the south-west face of Everest (1975).[97] He wrote three books: *Eiger Direct* (with Peter Gillman), *In High Places* and *Calculated Risk*, a posthumously published novel.

The name MacSporran – Gaelic *Mac an Sporain* – translates as 'Son of the Purse' and preserves the tradition of the clan's medieval role as hereditary purse-bearers, or treasurers, to Clan Donald. At least one Kintyre family adopted the name Pursell (no. 39), but that name has disappeared locally, while McSporran remains in strength.

The name Blue in Kintyre is an anglicisation of the Gaelic *Mac Gille Ghuirm* – in the old records 'McIlgurm', 'McIlgorm', etc – which is usually translated 'son of the blue lad', though the Rev William Matheson has pointed out that gorm can also mean 'raven-haired'. Whatever its original meaning, the name was earlier associated more with North Kintyre, and survives in County Antrim, by emigration, in the form 'McIlgorm'.[98] Indeed, the late actor and US President, Ronald Reagan, could claim Kintyre 'Blue blood' – his maternal great-grandmother was Jane Blue, a daughter of Donald Blue and Catherine MacFarlane. 'Blue the Baker's' – one of several local family-run baking businesses – was established in Campbeltown in 1870 and had premises at 2 and 46 Main Street between the wars. Alexander Blue, baker (died 30/6/1902, aged 55) and Thomas Blue, baker and confectioner (died 31/11/1937, aged 48) are buried in Kilkerran.

35. CARMICHAEL. Malcolm Carmichael (died 9/8/1919, Mafeking Place) is described as an 'Indian Mutiny Veteran'. This refers to the episode in colonial history – 1857–59 – when a revolt against British rule broke out in India, with the murder of officers and their families, and the beseiging of British garrisons (that at Cawnpore was massacred after surrendering).

Malcolm's first employment was as a gardener with Sir John Campbell of Auchinbreck, who resided at Kildalloig. Thereafter, he served for eight years as a soldier – his regiment is unknown, but may have been the 74th Highlanders[99] – and 'in later life . . . was very proud to be numbered among the veterans of the fighting days in the middle of last century'.

After military service, he returned to his native Campbeltown and to his previous occupation, and had charge of the gardens and grounds, successively, of South Park, Davaar House and East Cliff. He was 'a gardener of high attainment . . . possessing a great pride in his work', and was 'a most successful exhibitor at the local flower shows, and . . . a keen breeder of poultry'.[100]

Malcolm appears to have been born in 1840, to Malcolm Carmichael, fisherman, and Janet Mitchell. His wife Jane Swanston – died 10/4/1933, aged 82 – was born in Lauriston, Kincardine, and there is no evidence of a family. For remarks on Carmichael families in Kintyre, see no. 5.

36. WAREHAM. Before the twentieth century – and, in particular, before the Second World War, when Campbeltown hosted a substantial naval establishment – there was negligible English presence here, temporarily stationed Customs and Excise officers aside (no. 10). Wareham, however, represents a surname which goes back to a nineteenth century English seaman, James Wareham, about whom, unfortunately, little or nothing is known, except that he married Helen McKay, born 7/7/1813 in Campbeltown, daughter of Archibald McKay, carpenter, and Janet McCallum. James, interred here with his wife, Sarah Morrison, was a son of James Wareham and Mary Morrison and a grandson of the original James. He died 29/02/1948, aged 91. The family intermarried widely in the fishing community and became prominent boat-owners in Campbeltown in the twentieth century. John Wareham was a partner in the boat-owning consortium headed by Robert Robertson (no. 29), and skippered the ring-netters *Kestrel* and *Kittiwake* with notable success.

37. MCGEACHY. This is one of the local names – McIlchere is another – the pronunciation of which visitors find daunting. John Edward McGeachy (died 20/12/1943, aged 64) belonged to the McGeachy fishing family in Dalintober, which arrived there from Gigha in 1864. John Edward's father was Edward, but in the McGeachy family – originally from mainland Kintyre – 'Edward' represents Gaelic *Iomhar*, pronounced 'Eevar' and usually written 'Iver' or 'Ivor', e.g. Ivir mcGechie in Lergiebane in 1692, Ivor McGeachy in Kilkivan in 1750 and Iver MacGeachy in Beachmore in 1830. Another unusual male forename associated with the Dalintober McGeachys is 'Sweeney', for Gaelic *Suibhne*, which was probably collected on Gigha from the MacQuilkan family (Gaelic *Mac Cuilcein*, anglicised as Wilkinson). Sweeney, through intermarriage, later appeared in the Johnston and Wareham fishing families.

The McGeachy (*Mac Eachaidh*) family in Dalintober fished herring with notable success in the early twentieth century with the skiffs *White Heather*, *Isa McGeachy*, *Nancy*, *Una* and *Nemo*. A descendant of that family, John Martyn – born Iain McGeachy in 1948 – has distinguished himself in the world of contemporary music. A highly respected singer, guitarist and composer, among his many musical collaborators, and admirers, may be mentioned Stevie Winwood and Phil Collins, and among his numerous compositions, 'Bless the Weather', 'Solid Air' and 'May You Never', which Eric Clapton covered on his *Slowhand* album (1977).[101] Martyn, who has never enjoyed the commercial success which has fallen to lesser talents, is now based in Southern Ireland.

Local shoemaker, Sweeney McGeachy (died 1969, aged 82), was a master model boat-builder. A perfect scale model of the Loch Fyne Skiff *Fairy Queen* has been on display in Campbeltown Museum since 1952, and another of his models – the 1930s ringer *Nobles* – is

in the Science Museum, London, while several others are in private ownership. A fuller appreciation of his talents appears in *The Campbeltown Book*.[102]

John Edward McGeachy's wife, Janet McPhee (died 6/4/1934, aged 57), was a daughter of Duncan McPhee, farm servant at West Darlochan, and granddaughter of Duncan McPhee, a thatcher born c 1812 in Islay, and Janet McWilliam, born Drum, Killean Parish. The local business, Duncan McPhee, at Burnside Garage, represents that same family. MacPhee also appeared in the forms 'Duffie', 'MacDuff', etc. In 1816, in Campbeltown Parish, the baptism of Margaret, daughter of 'Hugh McDuff or McFie' and Catharine Montgomery, was recorded.

38. DOYLE. Though a Carruth stone – his daughter's married name – Hugh Doyle, 'Veteran of the Zulu War', is buried here, with his wife Mary Ann Edwards. He died 20/12/1936, aged 80, and was accorded a brief obituary in *The Campbeltown Courier* of 26/12/1936, which, unfortunately, gives no indication as to what brought him to Campbeltown, because there is no evidence that he was born here or had an early connection here, though his name points to Ireland.

The unprovoked imperialist invasion of Zululand was launched in

1879 and, following early military setbacks, culminated in the defeat of King Cetshwayo's forces at Ulundi on 4 July of that year, after which Zululand was partitioned and then ceased to exist.

Hugh's obituary concentrated on an illustrious, but impetuous, fellow-soldier, Prince Louis Napoleon: 'The ex-Prince Imperial of France, who with his father, the Emperor Napoleon III, had found refuge in Britain after the proclamation of the French Republic, served in the Zulu War in the unit in which the late Mr Doyle held the rank of Sergeant. Mr Doyle saw much of the unfortunate Prince, who was ambushed and killed by the Zulus [on 2 June, 1879], and had many thrilling stories to tell of the campaign.' Mrs Gloria Siggins believes that Hugh most likely served with the 17th Lancers, which regiment retrieved the Prince's corpse.[103]

39. PURSELL. This name, in Kintyre, is a logical anglicisation of Gaelic *Mac an Sporain*, 'Son of the Purse' (No. 34). Edward Pursell (died 5/5/1918, aged 67) was born in Campbeltown, son of Peter Pursell, flesher, and Mary Ramsay, and established a furniture and upholstery business – Pursell and Hall – in Longrow. His wife Mary Russell (1858–1955) was locally born of Lanarkshire parents, Robert Russell – farmer in Balliemenach, Kildalloig – and Mary Pettigrew. Robert, who came to Tirfergus at the age of nine with his father, took the tenancy of Ballymenach at the age of 24 and farmed there for exactly half-a-century, his son William taking over the lease. He died in 1912, at the age of 86, having outlived his wife by some 40 years.[104]

Two of Campbeltown's best-known footballers, Peter and Bobby Pursell, came from this marriage. Peter, while an amateur with Queen's Park, was capped for Scotland at full international level on 28 February, 1914, against Wales, at Celtic Park, Glasgow, a match which ended in a goal-less draw. (International football was suspended thereafter for the duration of the Great War.) He later signed for Glasgow Rangers and had a distinguished professional career. Bobby too played for Queen's Park and was capped for Amateur Scotland before joining Liverpool to play professionally.[105]

Edward Pursell (1891–1964), another son, recovered a vital part of his Gaelic heritage by learning the language. In 1950, that learning experience was to benefit countless others when the first course for Gaelic learners – of his devising – was broadcast by the BBC. He composed the popular song *Fàgail Liosmór* ('Leaving Lismore'), was crowned Mod Bard in 1946, became an accomplished landscape painter and was a keen gardener at Davaar House, for several years in succession winning the overall championship of the Campbeltown Horticultural Society Show.

Edward was educated at Campbeltown Grammar School, of which he was Dux and Kintyre Club Medallist in 1909, and at Glasgow University, whence he graduated MA. After completing his teacher-training, he taught at Oban High School, Dunoon Grammar School, and Tighnabruaich School (as headmaster) before, in 1932, returning to Campbeltown to become headmaster of Kinloch School – then the largest primary school in Argyll – in which post he remained until his retirement 24 years later. In 1924, he married Catriona Campbell of Oban, who died in 1956 and with whom he is buried in Oban. His second wife was Catherine Campbell, Lochawe. He had three sons and two daughters by his first marriage.[106]

A daughter, Iona, married Hector MacNeill MA (1918–98), a native Gaelic speaker who was born into a farming family in Knapdale and who followed Edward Pursell as headmaster of Kinloch School. During the Second World War, in HMS *Hotspur*, Hector saw active service in the battles of Narvik, Matapan and Crete, and in the period 1945–46 commanded the frigate HMS *Keats*. His hobbies included woodworking, climbing and gardening.[107]

Barra aside, Clan MacNeill in medieval times was strong in Gigha, Knapdale and Bute. In Kintyre, the MacNeills of Carskey appear on record in the early sixteenth century, followed by a branch in Tirfergus and Lossit, which later adopted the spelling 'Macneal' and to which belonged Hector MacNeill (1746–1818), famous in his time as a poet ('My Boy Tammie', 'Come under my Plaidie', etc).[108] James McNeill, headmaster of Drumlemble School from 1912 to 1939 and author of the idiosyncratic but rewarding *A Meander Round South Kintyre and Tales of Old Times*, first published in 1976, was born and died (in 1956) at Machrihanish. The MacNeills of Cushendun and Ballycastle, in County Antrim, Ireland, descend from Lachlan Buidhe of Tirfergus.[109] Several MacNeill families in nineteenth century Campbeltown were of Irish immigrant origin.

Partick-born Seumas MacNeill (1917–96) – physicist, piper, author, and Principal of the College of Piping, Glasgow – was taught piping by his Gigha uncle, the 'Blind Piper' Archie MacNeill, composer of the famous march, 'Donald MacLean's Farewell to Oban'.[110]

Division 4

40. MACCALLUM. Close to the east wall, which overlooks Kilkerran farmhouse, yet another MacCallum gravestone, this one leading us further into the world of piping and to a family which has produced a succession of skilled musicians, some MacCallum by name and others by blood relationship. This stone was erected by William MacCallum (died 25/05/1958, aged 68) and his wife Margaret McMurchy (died 22/8/1975, aged 77). Their son Hugh and grandson William (son of William Jr) rank among the foremost exponents of the bagpipe in the post-war period. To list, here, their numerous major prizes as solo competitors would mean little to the average reader, but within the piping fraternity the name MacCallum is synonymous with excellence.

William, commemorated on the gravestone, earned his living as a gardener, but he was a piper, too, as was his father, Pipe Major Ronald MacCallum. Ronald or Ranald is a typical Clan Donald name and ultimately derives from Old Norse *Rögnvaldr*. It entered the family of piping MacCallums through intermarriage with an earlier noted piping family, the MacAlisters, which originated in the Clachan area.

In 1845, William MacCallum (born 1823, at Balloch, son of Archibald MacCallum, thatcher, and Mary Ryburn) married Mary MacAlister (born 1826, at Kilkerran, daughter of Ronald MacAlister, weaver, and Mary McKellar). In June, 1858, William, a mason, was badly maimed when a cannon he was helping reload exploded prematurely during the marriage celebrations of Duncan Stewart, his employer's son, which accident rendered him unemployable in his trade.[111]

The name McMurchy too has a piping connection in Kintyre, albeit in an earlier period. William MacMurchy, who died about 1778, was piper to MacDonald of Largie, and also wrote Gaelic poetry. The MacMurchy name – also recorded as MacMurphy and shortened as Murphy – has a complex background and could represent either *Mac Mhurchaidh* or *Mac Mhuirich*, or both. The

Kintyre connections of the distinguished *Mac Mhuirich* bardic line – hereditary poets and historians to Clan Donald – are examined in my ***Kintyre: The Hidden Past***.[112] The Drumlemble poet, James McMurchy (1835–1909), was both 'MacMurphy' and 'Murphy' at various times[113], and offshoots of his family in North America who used the form 'Murphy' subsequently adopted 'McMurchy' to identify themselves as Protestants.[114]

41. NEWLANDS. Against the west wall, among other members of the family, Duncan Inglis Newlands, celebrated coxswain of Campbeltown lifeboat, who died 2/11/1979, aged 83. Duncan joined the RNLI around 1921; in 1933 he became bowman, in 1939 second coxswain and in 1944 coxswain, which position he held until his retirement in 1961. His service – 100 rescues and more than 300 lives saved – brought him the RNLI Bronze Medal in 1942, to which was added a clasp for the rescue of the crew and passengers of the American liberty ship, *Byron Darnton*, which grounded off Sanda on 16 March, 1946, one of Coxswain Newlands' dramatic exploits which Angus MacVicar described in ***Rescue Call*** (1967). In 1953, he was awarded a Queen's Coronation Medal.

Duncan left school at 13 and became a trainee fisherman, or

Coxwain Duncan Newlands rescuing from the American liberty ship 'cook', with the Gilchrist family; but after service in the Royal Naval Volunteer Reserve during the 1914–18 war, he never returned to full-time fishing. He became, however, a boat-owner – first with the *Verbena* and then with the *May Allan* – conducting fishing trips and carrying visitors to Davaar Island. It was during a trip to the island that he met a holidaymaker, Jamesina Cruikshank, who became his wife in 1931. She belonged to Kilbarchan, Renfrewshire, where her father James – a native of Macduff – was employed as a gardener. She died in 1950, aged 46, and is buried with her parents, who retired to Campbeltown.

Duncan also operated the lighthouse tender to Davaar Island, was relief light-keeper there and worked as a stevedore on Campbeltown Quay, in which connection he was a founder-member of the local branch of the Transport & General Workers' Union. His daughter, May, who became a teacher of music at Campbeltown Grammar School, married Harry McIver in 1958.[115]

I visited Duncan in 1974, while researching my first book, *The Ring-Net Fishermen*. My first mistake was to tap his barometer, a practice of which he decidedly did not approve! My second mistake was to produce a tape-recorder, of which, regrettably, he also did not approve; so I had to settle for an informal, and less rewarding, interview.

Duncan Newlands' paternal grandparents were Irish: John Knowland – this spelling from his marriage certificate: the various forms in nineteenth century Campbeltown total at least 10, all, however, representing Irish Ó *Nualláin* – and Nancy Lynn, Irish Ó *Fhloinn*, born in County Antrim. For information on the several Newlands families in Campbeltown, see my *Kintyre: The Hidden Past*.[116] Duncan's mother, Catherine Sharp, a 29-year-old farm servant at Kildalloig when she married George Newlands on 28/11/1893, was a daughter of James Sharp, fisherman, and Catherine Fowler.

Division 6

42. LANG. Malcolm McNeill Lang (died 21/1/1990, aged 85), a son of Peter Lang and Rosina Campbell, founded a reputable plumbing business in Campbeltown, employing three of his sons, Peter, Dougie and David. Another son, Ian (1932–2003), is remem-

· LANG ·

8 YEAR OLD
CATHERINE AND
THE MERMAID.

bered locally as a championship-winning drum-major. Among his
successes may be mentioned the Scottish championship in 1960, at
Princes Street Gardens, Edinburgh, and the World title at Murray-
field Stadium, Edinburgh, in 1961. Malcolm's wife, Jean Morrison
(died 16/10/1992, aged 85), was a daughter of John Morrison,
distillery workman, and Catherine McKendrick.

The name Lang in Kintyre represents an anglicisation of
O'Loynachan and Loynachan, variously spelt in old records.
Malcolm was descended from a branch of the family which tenanted
the Learside farm of Balinatunie, near Auchenhoan, in the early
nineteenth century. These Loynachans were related to the branch –
at Shennachie, Glenehervie – which produced the girl (born 1810)
who inspired the nineteenth century song, 'Flory Loynachan', still
sung and recited locally. Flory's sister, Mary (born 1813), enjoyed
a different kind of celebrity in Canada, where she attained her
hundredth birthday.

In 1811, eight-year-old Catherine Loynachan, daughter of
Lachlan, claimed to have seen a mermaid while herding cattle on the
shore near Balinatunie.[117] Duncan Loynachan, father of Lachlan
Loynachan, boatbuilder in Campbeltown, was born at Balinatunie
around 1808.

One of the descendants of the Balinatunie Loynachans, David S MacArthur, a schoolteacher, wrote short stories, plays for radio and television, and a novel *The Thunderbolt Men*. He was born in Campbeltown in 1910 to Thomas MacArthur and Lizzie Lang.

O'Loynachan was one of many names of the Ó type in seventeenth century Kintyre. O'May – an interesting old Kintyre family which in both pre-Reformation and post-Reformation times produced many clerics[118] – is the last remaining native Kintyre surname with the prefix O, denoting 'grandson of'. Of *Mac* – 'son of' – there are, of course, numerous instances in Kintyre, throughout Scotland, and, indeed, the world; but O is now almost exclusively associated with Irish surnames, of which, in Campbeltown, O'Hara is now the only one. Some of these seventeenth century O names remain in the community, but have been anglicised unrecognisably. As 'O'Loynachan' became Lang, so 'O'Kaldie' became Kelly, while many others – such as 'Ocolchan', 'Ocholtan', 'Ocoyne', 'Odiman' and 'Obriann', to quote the crude anglicised forms of the time – completely disappeared soon afterwards.

43. MITCHELL. As the exhortation at the foot of the stone – 'SING A SANG AT LEAST' – proclaims, this is the grave of a singer, among other attributes. Willie Mitchell (died 28/01/1986) was a musician as well as singer, but more significantly he collected and preserved folksongs in Kintyre and wrote both poems and songs. The best-known of his compositions is unquestionably 'Road to Drumlemman', which is sung – and recorded – world-wide.

A butcher to trade, Willie was an avid cyclist and walker before these 'leisure activities' became so fashionable. The epic walk of his life didn't have its starting-point in China or the Arctic. It started right here in Campbeltown, at 6 o' clock one morning in 1929, and he walked to Machrihanish, south to the Mull, through Southend and up the Learside. As he passed the Rocky Burn, on his final mile, and after 18 hours of foot-slogging, the old Victoria Hall clock was chiming midnight.[119] That feat has, to my knowledge, never been attempted, far less emulated.

Willie's paternal ancestors – Duncan Mitchell and Mary McConnachie – can be traced to the eighteenth century in Torrisdale Glen, where a son of theirs, also Duncan, married my great-great grandfather's sister, Isabella Martin. These Martins later migrated to

Willie Mitchell in the early 1970's

MITCHELL

Dalintober, established themselves as fishermen and boat-owners, and were joined in the enterprise by Duncan Mitchell, whose family too settled in Dalintober.

Andy Mitchell, born in 1945 in Boddam, Aberdeenshire, and now living on Skye, has continued the family's musical tradition. Willie and Andy's father, the Rev Duncan Mitchell, were full cousins, but Duncan was born and brought up in Carradale. Andy's best-known composition, 'Indiana', has appeared on some thirty albums at the last count.

A grandson of Willie Mitchell's, Fergus Mitchell Kerr (born 1972), has been making a name for himself professionally on the French Horn. A son of teachers John Kerr and Cathy Mitchell, who married in 1966, Fergus started on the instrument at the age of eight, studying under Gordon Evans. Having embarked on a career in engineering, he then dedicated himself to music and spent two years as a post-graduate student at the Royal Scottish Academy of Music and Drama. His folk background, however, has not been erased by engagement with classical music; as a member of 'Strings Attached' – which also included the five Scottish fiddlers known as 'Blazin Fiddles' – he appeared at the 2006 Celtic Connections festival in Glasgow.

Though presumably of Lowland settler-stock originally, these Torrisdale Mitchells were certainly Gaelic-speaking and must, there-fore, have been assimilated into the Gaelic culture which prevailed outwith southern Kintyre, as were branches of such other Lowland families as Armour, Colville and Wallace, all Gaelic-speaking by the nineteenth century.[120] Consider, however, that 'McIlmichel' (Gaelic *Mac Ghille Mhicheil*), which in Kintyre became 'Carmichael', mutated into 'Mitchell' in parts of Mid Argyll.[121]

Willie Mitchell's wife, Agnes R Morrison (died 29/8/1988, aged 88), came from a family of crofter-fishermen which lived at Pluck, north of Saddell, in the nineteenth century, though originally from Campbeltown Parish. Morrisons – some of them, at least, originally 'McVorran', Gaelic *Mac Mhoirein* – are recorded throughout Kintyre from the seventeenth century onward. In the Old Parish Registers for Campbeltown, 10/3/1817, Charles was registered son of Donald McVorran and Anne Martin.

Division 3

44. STEWART. On the way out, against the wall and south of the burn, this modest and enigmatic memorial – 'In Memory of/ Archibald Stewart/ A True Friend/ From the Tarbert Fishermen' – with its perfect images of a herring and a ring-net boat, marks the grave of Archibald Stewart, Procurator-Fiscal of Campbel-town, who was killed during the German air-raid on the town on 9 February, 1941. His father, John, had been a fisherman in Campbeltown, hence Archibald's empathy with the fishing community and his legal service to fishermen, often freely rendered.

Author Naomi Mitchison, back in Carradale after an absence, remarks in her Mass-Observation diary on 22 February 1941: 'They are all talking about the raid on Campbeltown and Stewart's death; apparently it was a land-mine. He wasn't killed outright but died of wounds.' She added that her secretary at Carradale, Rosemary Jones, who witnessed the massively attended funeral, remarked that 'she had never seen so many men crying as there were at his funeral.'[122]

Archibald's son, Archibald Ian Balfour Stewart (1915–98) – popularly known as 'AIB' or 'Ian' – joined his father in the firm of Stewart, Balfour & Sutherland, having graduated Bachelor of Law, with distinction, from Glasgow University in 1938. Following his father's sudden death, Ian found himself, at the age of 25, both head of the law practice and Procurator-Fiscal of Campbeltown, a position he held until 1974. Like his father, he had a keen interest in the fishing industry. Secretary of the Clyde Fishermen's Association until 1974, and instrumental, in 1973, in the founding of the Scottish Fishermen's Federation, of which he was the first president, he was active at the highest level of fisheries politics, which services brought him an OBE (1966) and CBE (1975). His hobbies included philately, his particular expertise being in the postmarks of the French army.[123]

Ian, who was born in Campbeltown and educated both at Campbeltown Grammar School and Cheltenham College, was also an industrious local historian and genealogist, with many published articles to his name. He was an active member of the Kintyre Antiquarian and Natural History Society, of which he was president and editor of its bi-annual journal, *The Kintyre Magazine*. His painstaking transcription of the *List of Inhabitants upon the Duke of Argyle's property in Kintyre in 1792*, published in 1991, liberated a veritable treasury of genealogical data. In 1944, he married Ailsa Massey. They had three sons, all of whom followed him into the legal profession, Patrick and John to the family practice and Angus to the Bar.

Ian's paternal grandparents, John Stewart (died 10/2/1884, aged 41) and Barbara Thomson (died 5/11/1882, aged 40) are buried in Kilkivan. She was a daughter of Archibald Thomson – of the Drumlemble family which produced a succession of professional golfers – and Margaret Morrison.

Ian's great-grandfather, Coll Stewart, who married Martha McCallum of Saddell, was a native of Lismore Island. He was the son of John Stewart and Mary Livingstone of Bachuil. The Livingstones of Bachuil are hereditary keepers of the pastoral staff, or *bachuil*, of Saint Moluag (died 592). The *bachuil* is reputed to have been one of the relics paraded before the Scottish army at Bannockburn. The explorer, Dr David Livingstone, and Donald 'Mollach' Livingstone of Savary, Morven, who rescued the Appin Stewarts' banner (now in the National Museums of Scotland) from the field of Culloden, are said to be of that same family.[124]

The Duke of Argyll's chamberlain in Kintyre from 1791, Duncan Stewart, Esq, of Glenbuckie, married into the Stewarts of Ardshiel. That family suffered heavy losses at Culloden – eight members killed and three wounded – and Ardshiel himself was attainted of high treason, but escaped and died in France. The Glenbuckie Stewarts also suffered for the Jacobite cause, John Glas Stewart of Benmore and two of his nephews being killed at Culloden, and Alexander, his uncle, at Killiecrankie. The Glenbuckie Stewarts trace their lineage from Murdoch Stewart (c. 1362–1425), 2nd Duke of Albany and Regent of Scotland. Duncan Stewart's son, John Lorne Stewart of Coll (1800–78), was born at Limecraigs, Campbeltown, and, having succeeded to the chamberlainship of Kintyre after his father's death in 1828, became a noted agricultural improver in Kintyre,[125] at the expense, however, of his popularity with the Duke's tenant-farmers.

For information on other Kintyre Stewart families, see AIB Stewart's 'Some Kintyre Stewarts'[126] and David Jackson's 'The Rev Alexander Stewart (1755–1798) of the Kintyre "Park" Stewarts: Facts and Hearsay'.[127]

Some Campbeltown Stewarts stem from nineteenth century Irish immigration, including Archibald 'Baldy' Stewart, a notable fisherman and 'character'. His grandparents were Campbell Stewart – born in County Down – and Catherine McLellan, daughter of Archibald McLellan and Mary McAulay. 'Baldy' (1897–1974) married into a local fishing family, the McNaughtons. His wife, May (1893–1948), was a daughter of David McNaughton and Maria Robertson, whose father was the Dalintober ferryman, James Robertson.

'Baldy' was one of the skippers employed in the Robertson boat-owning consortium (no. 29), but had the ring-netter *Boy Danny* built in 1948 for himself and his four sons, Archibald, William, Charles and David. He was awarded the British Empire Medal for his part in the rescue of the crew of a Sunderland of 228 Squadron which crashed at Lochboisdale on 4 May, 1942[128], and was among the survivors when the pleasure-boat *Quesada* foundered off Davaar Island in May, 1966.

APPENDIX

Christian Names

Apropos Montgomery (no. 19), other unusual local female Christian names deriving from surnames would include Crichton, Douglas and Hamilton, and unusual male Christian names would certainly include Fleming McNaughton (born 1861); his son Smollet (born 1889); Pinkerton Martin (born c. 1774); Scipio McKinven (born c. 1843); Naismith McPherson Jr. (fl. 1898); Beatty Pownall Mansefield (born 1890, and obviously named in honour of Colonel G. A. Beaty-Pownall, Argyll & Bute Militia adjutant from 1875–81), and Proudfoot McIntyre (born c. 1896, and presumably named from an Inland Revenue officer, Patrick MacFarlane Proudfoot, who died in 1856 and is buried in the old section).

Douglas Bruce McKinlay of Dalintober received his call-up papers at the very end of the Second World War and joined the Highland Light Infantry, in which he served for nearly three years. After he'd written out the obligatory will, the military authorities contacted his mother pointing out that he'd named himself as the beneficiary, and enquiring if, as Douglas himself put it, he was 'right in the head'. His mother fired off a 'sharp reply', pointing out that she too was Douglas Bruce McKinlay![129] Her own surname was McKinnon and I believe her other names must come from Douglas Bruce – born in 1798 in Saddell and Skipness Parish – who married Charles Shaw.

Christian names which have a topical or impulsive origin are seldom wisely chosen. Perhaps the most bizarre I have come across in Campbeltown commemorated two First World War battles – Verdun Loos McLellan, born 29/5/1916, died 1/12/1918 – and I'm not at all certain that the Durnan girl, born 23/8/1872 and registered Janet, would have thanked her mother for changing her name, three years later, by deposition, to Vincent Ceni Celetti, in honour of the

Italian priest who came to St Kieran's RC Church, Campbeltown, in 1868.

The generality of Christian names, however, were drawn from a fairly stable fund and recur generation after generation, often in a rigid pattern, so that the first-born son will be named after his father's father, the second after his mother's father, and then after paternal and maternal uncles in turn; and the same with daughters, except that the precedence is maternally-based, starting with the mother's mother. This pattern is often helpful in establishing connections when a cluster of same-name births occurs within a narrow time-scale.

The various ethnic groups in Kintyre tended to exhibit characteristic forenames, at least until the twentieth century, by which time native, Lowland and Irish families were intermarrying extensively and exchanging forenames. Thus, the native, or Highland, families abound in Gaelic names, such as *Alasdair* (Alexander), *Aonghas* (Angus), *Cailean* (Colin), *Calum* (Malcolm), *Domhnall* (Donald), and *Eachunn* (Hector), whereas the Lowlanders are distinguishable by such names as Andrew, David, Gavin, Lionel, Mathew, Nathaniel, and common others – e.g. James, John, Robert, and William – which also had their Gaelic and Irish counterparts. Characteristic Irish male forenames include Anthony, Denis, Daniel, Francis, Hugh, Michael and Patrick. Patrick is also, however, found within the early Lowland stock, and Daniel was widely used as a native equivalent of Domhnall, whereas Hugh – of Norman origin – was used by all three groups, serving as the anglicised form of three Gaelic/Irish names, of which *Eòghann* was the native one. So, as these three examples alone show, the distinctions are far from simple.

Female Christian names are less varied, and relatively few are recognisably Gaelic, but, as with male names, most of the old Gaelic names were either dropped or anglicised. Morag – diminutive of *Mór* – is one of the few authentic Gaelic female names still current; Sarah was its Biblical substitute. Ishbel is the anglicised form of Gaelic *Iseabail*, which derives, however, from Isabel, originally a Spanish form of Elizabeth, and there are many such borrowings into Gaelic. Mirren – still remembered among the elderly – was replaced with the similar-sounding Marion. Efric is an anglicisation of the Norse-derived *Oighrig*, which in the Western Isles was invariably written as Euphemia or Henrietta and shortened to 'Effie' and 'Etta'.

Senga is usually classed as Scottish and explained as representing 'Agnes' backwards, but *The Oxford Names Companion* prefers to derive it from Gaelic *seang*, 'slender'.[130] During a voyage to the Marquesas, Paul Theroux met 'a woman from Chicago who called herself Senga (she hated the name Agnes and so spelled it backwards) . . .'[131]

The female form of Gavin is rare, but one Gavina Ralston Conner died at Louth, Lincolnshire, on 28 December, 2004. Gavina is hardly a typical 'ina' name, however, requiring only the terminal 'a'. These often clumsy 'ina' conversions of male into female forenames, though never locally common, have fortunately declined, because the bearers often detested such monstrosities as Williamina, Robertina, Alexandrina, Roderickina and Jamesina, and chose to be known as simply 'Ina' or instead used a middle name, if they had one.

Some Christian names are particularly associated with certain families. In the Campbells, Colin and Walter recur frequently, the latter perhaps deriving from the mid-sixteenth century Walter Campbell of Skipness, forebear of the Campbells of Islay; Lawrence appeared in one of the McKinven families and passed into the Robertsons through marriage; Maurice/Morris (probably from the Irish *Muirgheos*) seems to appear as a McSporran name, and spread, by intermarriage, into such other local families as the McIntyres and McNairs. The mother of Morris McIntyre – well-known Campbeltown fitness enthusiast and custodian of local civic values, who died on 19 December, 2004 – was Jane McSporran.

REFERENCES AND NOTES

In these references and notes, *Argyllshire Advertiser* is abbreviated to *AA*, *Argyllshire Herald* to *AH*, *Campbeltown Courier* to *CC*, *The Kintyre Magazine* to *KM*, and Registers of Poor, Campbeltown Parish, to RP.

1. Edinburgh 1995, p 65.
2. *CC*, 23/2/1929, 'Kilkerran Cemetery: History of the Various Divisions'.
3. *AH*, 22/5/1869.
4. *CC*, 2/1/1884.
5. *AH*, 23/3/1878.
6. *Glasgow Herald*, 21/5/1821.
7. *A Ramble Through the Old Kilkerran Graveyard*, 1922, p 12.
8. RP 195, 30/10/1860.
9. *AH*, 5/10/1860.
10. A Martin, *Kintyre:The Hidden Past*, Edinburgh 1984, p 209; R MacilleDhuibh, 'The Horse People of Kintyre', *KM* No. 36, pp 12–17.
11. A Martin, *Kintyre Country Life*, Edinburgh 1987, pp 62–3.
12. KA Steer & JWM Bannerman, *Late Medieval Monumental Sculpture in the West Highlands*, Edinburgh 1977, pp 159–60 & pp 157–58.
13. H Campbell (Ed), *Miscellany of the Scottish History Society*, Edinburgh 1926, pp 200–4.
14. *CC*, 7/6/1902.
15. Quoted in *CC*, 12/4 & 3/5/1924.
16. *AH*, 22/5/1869.
17. *Kintyre: The Hidden Past*, *op. cit.*, p 214.
18. *CC*, 8/1/1927.
19. *Op. cit.*, p 214.
20. A Martin, *Kintyre: The Hidden Past*, *op. cit.*, p 75. See also E R Cregeen, 'The MacKeith Family at Kilmichael', *KM* No. 50, pp 28–31.
21. Bill McKeich, *KM* No. 59, p 29.
22. A Martin, *St Kieran's RC Church, Campbeltown: A Parish History, 1850–2000*; unpublished.
23. G Siggins, 'Tragedy in Archangel – The Killing of John Allan Watson', *KM* No. 52, pp 2–6.
24. Letters to author from Joyce Perry, grand-daughter of H Grantham, 26/1/1995, 2/2/1995 & 17/8/2004.

25. M MacDonald, Archivist, letter to author, 16/8/2004.
26. D O McEwan, *Wings of Faith: A History of Saint Kiaran's Scottish Episcopal Church, Campbeltown*, Edinburgh 2003, p 8.
27. A McKerral, *Kintyre in the Seventeenth Century*, Edinburgh 1948, p 174; D Kelly, *CC*, 14/4/2006.
28. *CC*, 23/10/1909.
29. M MacDonald, *The Campbeltown Book*, Campbeltown 2003, p 310.
30. *CC*, 11/3/1871.
31. H Scott, *Fasti Ecclesiae Scoticanae*, Vol 14, Edinburgh 1923, pp 120–21.
32. M Davidson, 'George Thomas Beatson, KCB, KBE, MD, DL', *KM* No. 49, pp 16–19.
33. A Campbell of Airds, letter to author, 7/10/2004.
34. Mactaggart family private papers.
35. *CC*, obit of John, 14/5/1892; of William, *ibid.*, 27/8/1887; annual Calendars of Confirmations and Inventories for wills.
36. A Campbell of Airds, letter to author, 18/10/04.
37. A McKerral, *Kintyre in the Seventeenth Century*, op. cit., pp 97–98.
38. *AH*, obit, 16/1/1897.
39. Mrs Marion Wallace Reid, letters to author, 8 & 24/8/2004.
40. A Martin, *KM* No. 50, p 19.
41. H Scott, *Fasti Ecclesiae Scoticanae*, op. cit., p 53.
42. *CC*, 9/2/1924.
43. Mrs B Macmillan Wilkie, letter to author, 5 June 2005.
44. *Ibid.*
45. *Op. cit.*, p 152.
46. *Kintyre in the Seventeenth Century*, op. cit., p 167.
47. A Martin, *KM* No. 37, p 32.
48. *CC*, 22/2/1908.
49. Mrs B Macmillan Wilkie, letter, op. cit.
50. *Family History Monthly*, April 2004.
51. *The Herald*, 4/10/1996.
52. *Ibid.*
53. A Martin, *KM* No. 37, p 30.
54. Duncan C MacTavish, *Commons of Argyll*, Lochgilphead 1935, pp 3 & 47.
55. *Kintyre in the Seventeenth Century*, op. cit., p 174.
56. A Martin, *Kintyre: The Hidden Past*, op. cit., pp 199.
57. *Ibid.*, pp 212–13.
58. *CC*, 26/9/1914, obit of Mrs Peter MacKinnon.
59. *CC*, 18/2/1911, obit.
60. *CC*, 2/5/1931, 'Death of Mr William Young, Glencraig'.
61. Francis McWhirter, personal communication, 25/7/2004.
62. A Martin, *St Kieran's RC Church*, Campbeltown, op. cit.

63. D Grumoli Kennedy, 'The Italian Community in Campbeltown', *KM* No. 48, pp 4–12.
64. A Wilson, *The Herald*, obit, 14/9/1996.
65. P Pugh, *Is Guinness Good for You?*, London 1987, p 64.
66. A Wilson, *op. cit.*
67. *The Encyclopaedia of Modern History*, London 1978, p 194.
68. *CC*, 7/8/1915.
69. G Siggins, letters to author, 8/2004.
70. A Martin, *KM* No. 37, pp 30–31.
71. A Martin, *Ibid.*, No. 56, p 26.
72. *CC*, 17/1/1880.
73. Scottish Record Office, E326 10/1 & 10/7.
74. Entry 1557.
75. *CC*, 25/12/1909.
76. RP, entry 1994.
77. *Ibid.*, entry 1270.
78. J Rafferty, *One Hundred Years of Scottish Football*, London 1973, pp 169, 186, 203.
79. A McKinven, *KM* No. 48, p 29.
80. *CC*, 12/1/1935.
81. A Martin, 'Travelling People in Kintyre', unpublished article; H Henderson, 'The Tinkers', in *A Companion to Scottish Culture*, ed D Daiches, London 1981; D Whyte, *Scottish Gypsies and other Travellers*, Alfreton 2001.
82. Ian MacDonald, letter to author, 2/2/2002.
83. *AA*, 4/5/1949.
84. A Martin, *The Ring-Net Fishermen*, Edinburgh 1981, pp 211–19.
85. RP, entries 969 and 1061 (Robertson) and 1286 (Mathieson).
86. 'H.E. Clifford, Architect', *The Campbeltown Book*, *op. cit.*, 281–295.
87. K McNeil, *Ibid.*
88. D Stevenson, *Alasdair MacColla and the Highland problem in the 17th Century*, Edinburgh 1980, p 159.
89. A Martin, *St Kieran's RC Church, Campbeltown*, *op. cit.*
90. P Berresford Ellis, *Erin's Royal Blood*, New York 2002, p 253.
91. *AH*, 23/12/1899, obit.
92. A Campbell of Airds, letter to author, 7/10/2004.
93. KA Steer & JWM Bannerman, *op. cit.*, pp 156–57.
94. A Martin, *Kintyre:The Hidden Past*, *op. cit.*, pp 92–94 & 202.
95. A Martin, *ibid.*, p 13; A Martin, *Kintyre Country Life*, Edinburgh 1987, p 73; see also a feature on the life of George Todd Jr, *CC*, 31/12/1932.
96. J.B. White Ltd, Glenrothes, N.D.
97. J Connor, *Dugal Haston: The Philosophy of Risk*, Edinburgh 2002.
98. A Martin, *Kintyre: The Hidden Past*, *op. cit.*, pp 94 & 208.
99. Gloria Siggins, letter to author, 30/7/2004.
100. *CC*, 16/8/1919, obit.

101. M C Strong, *The Great Rock Discography*, Edinburgh 1998, pp 508–9.
102. A Martin, 'The Campbeltown Fishing Industry', *The Campbeltown Book*, *op. cit.*, p 82.
103. Letter to author, 30/7/2004.
104. *CC*, 18/5/1912, obit.
105. A McKinven, *op. cit.*, p 29; J Rafferty, *op. cit.*, p 202.
106. *CC*, obit, 13/2/1964.
107. *The Herald*, obit, 4/8/1998.
108. AIB Stewart, *KM* No. 20, pp 21–28.
109. R McDonnell, *The Glynns*, Vol 1, 1973, pp 21–24.
110. *West Highland Free Press*, obit, 12/4/1996.
111. A Martin, *Kintyre Country Life*, *op. cit.*, p 182; RP, entry 183, registered 25/9/1860.
112. *Op. cit.*, pp 6–8 & 213.
113. *Ibid.*, p 10.
114. R Booth, letter to author, 8/4/2006.
115. From family papers in possession of Mrs May McIver, 5/9/2004.
116. *Op. cit.*, p 205.
117. A Martin, *Kintyre: The Hidden Past*, *op. cit.*, pp 192.
118. AIB Stewart, *The Scottish Genealogist*, Vol XXX, No. 2, June 1983.
119. A Stewart, 'A Sang at Least: The Life of William Mitchell', *KM* No. 51, pp 2–11.
120. A Martin, *Kintyre: The Hidden Past*, *op. cit.*, p 34.
121. Marion Campbell, 'The Kilberry and Knockbuy Rentroll Books', Argyll & Bute Archive, unpublished.
122. *Among You Taking Notes . . . The Wartime Diary of Naomi Mitchison, 1939–1945*, ed D Sheridan, London 1985, p 122.
123. *The Herald*, 20/10/1998.
124. Angus Stewart, letter to author, 29/9/2004.
125. *The Celtic Monthly*, No. 2, Vol III, Nov 1894.
126. *The Scottish Genealogist*, Vol 41, No. 3, pp 97–102.
127. *KM* No. 52, pp 22–26.
128. A Martin, *The North Herring Fishing*, Colonsay 2001, p 156.
129. D McKinlay, personal communication, 6/9/2004.
130. Oxford 2002, p 862.
131. *The Happy Isles of Oceania*, London 1992, p 395.

INDEX OF FAMILY NAMES

In the interest of uniformity, all names which appear as *Mc-* in the main text are rendered *Mac* in this index. Original Gaelic and variant spellings of names are not listed. Likewise, individuals mentioned in the text – e.g. Robert Burns, Dougal Haston and J.K. Rowling – are not indexed.